The New Americans
Recent Immigration and American Society

Edited by
Steven J. Gold and Rubén G. Rumbaut

A Series from LFB Scholarly

Creating Black Caribbean Ethnic Identity

Yndia S. Lorick-Wilmot

LFB Scholarly Publishing LLC
El Paso 2010

Library of Congress Cataloging-in-Publication Data

Lorick-Wilmot, Yndia S., 1977-
   Creating black Caribbean ethnic identity / Yndia S. Lorick-Wilmot.
     p. cm. -- (The new Americans : recent immigration and American society)
   Includes bibliographical references and index.
   ISBN 978-1-59332-408-7 (hbk. : alk. paper)
   1. Caribbean Americans--Social conditions. 2. Caribbean Americans--Ethnic identity. 3. Caribbean Americans--Services for. 4. Caribbean Americans--New York (State)--New York--Social conditions. 5. Caribbean Americans--New York (State)--New York--Ethnic identity. 6. Caribbean Americans--Services for--New York (State)--New York. 7. Caribbean Service Center (Brooklyn, N.Y.) I. Title.
   E184.C27L66 2010
   305.896'0729--dc22
                             2010014571

ISBN 978-1-59332-408-7

Printed on acid-free 250-year-life paper.

Manufactured in the United States of America.

Table of Contents

Acknowledgments

For making my fieldwork possible, many thanks to The Caribbean Service Center's then executive director and staff, Founders, Board of Directors, community stakeholders, and clients for sharing their time, insight, and organization's records and facility. I learned so much about The Caribbean Service Center, its Caribbean immigrant clients and community. These participants sat and talked with me for hours and they shared interesting stories of resiliency, persistence, and triumph, which continue to inspire me.

I have been blessed with more than my fair share of great colleagues and friends. Since the project's inception, during my time in the Department of Sociology at Northeastern University, I am grateful to Winifred Breines, Maureen Kelleher, Paula Aymer, and Gordana Rabrenovic for their continuous support, keen advice, and constructive feedback. Their comments and expert guidance were invaluable to my finishing this project. Many thanks to Natasha Gordon-Chipembere, my copy editor and friend, whose enthusiasm and good heart inspire me and made it possible for me to bring this manuscript to press. I am also thankful for the friendships that endured and, in many ways, sustained me during all phases of my work. I benefited greatly from friends' comments on drafts of the work.

I would like to extend my deepest gratitude to my family, especially my parents Taecha and Curives, for their endless support, love, encouragement, and insightful commentary. To my children Justin and Sydney, I am thankful for their love and laughter. Finally, I am grateful to Damian, my husband and partner on this journey, for his critical comments, sense of humor, and support.

CHAPTER 1

Introduction

Bananas
Ripe and green, and ginger-root
Cocoa in pods and alligator pears
And tangerines and mangoes and grape fruit
Fit for the highest prize
At parish fairs

Set in the window, bringing memories
Of fruit-trees laden by low-singing rills
And dewy dawns, and mystical blue skies
In benediction over nun-like hills.

My eyes grew dim, and I could no more gaze;
A wave of longing through my body swept,
And, hungry for the old, familiar ways,
I turned aside and bowed my head and wept.

(Claude McKay, "The Tropics in New York")

Feelings of yearning, nostalgia, and mourning, often conveyed in the works of Jamaican-born poet Claude McKay, are common sentiments held by many immigrants who live and work in the United States. These sentiments help to keep alive the hope immigrants have of one day returning to their native countries. As time passes, however, immigrants develop ties to churches, social organizations, jobs, communities, and friends that anchor them here longer than they may have initially intended. While the generalization regarding immigrants' original intentions to remain in America may ring true for many, the process by which ethnic immigrants develop these ties is largely determined by a host of social and economic circumstances, particularly circumstances related to race and ethnicity, that influences their adaptation, acculturation, and ultimately their ethnic identity (Yoshikawa and Way 2008).

Since the passage of the Immigration Act of 1965, the increased presence and visibility of ethnic immigrants from Asia, Africa, and the Caribbean to the United States has had a growing demographic, political, cultural, and economic impact on American society. This increased visibility has generated a substantial body of research on the various ways these immigrants and their descendants are assimilated into American society (see Alba and Nee 2005; Berry and Phinney 2006; Hume 2008; Park 1950; Portes and Rumbaut 1990; Portes and Bach 1985; Ravage 1917; Znaniecki 1923; Waters 1994, 1999; Zhou 1998). Scholarship on the acculturation of racial-ethnic immigrants emphasize the importance of race, racial and ethnic identities, and their implications on first generation immigrant assimilation and its second generation's economic mobility (Benson 2006; Crowder and Tedrow 2001; Foner 2001; Rogers 2001; Waters 1999).

Unlike their European predecessors, scholars have argued racial-ethnic immigrants' experiences do not conform to the "classic" European model of ethnic assimilation and cultural accommodation. Robert Merton's notion of "master status"--which suggests there is one aspect of individuals' identity that society will draw on to define them-- can be used to illustrate this variation in the process of acculturation. For racial-ethnic groups, their master status is based on race. Recent sociology discourse recognizes race as a social construct and the assumption of its relevance to biology as the basis for America's racial system. Racial systems are ways of classifying people, usually by judging how closely their phenotype "fits" with physical descriptions of what different "races" look like. Because the United States is rooted in the European enslavement of African people, its racial classification system relegates those that have African-like features and/or dark skin color to lower social levels. Unfortunately, one's position within this race-based classification system determines a person's master status.

Many ethnic immigrant groups share similar experiences related to racial inclusion and exclusion as a result of their master status, yet scholars have argued that Caribbean people of Anglophone,

Francophone and Hispanophone ancestry bring with them a particular phenotype that result in their racial classification as Black. To be racially classified as Black or as having a Black master status limits Caribbean immigrants' ability to fully access opportunities in ways that non-Black ethnic immigrant groups are able to access them (Davis 1991). In particular, due to American society's history of racism toward individuals with varying shades of brown skin, these racial-ethnic immigrants and their children face a unique set of challenges in their efforts to acquire equal access to opportunities (e.g., occupational, educational, and residential) (Benson 2006). As a result, Caribbean immigrants learn very quickly how race and the implications of a Black master status have crucial consequences for their experiences (Benson 2006; Bryce-Laporte 1972; Foner 1987; Ho 1991; Zephir 1996).

Despite the determining power of a Black master status in the lives of Caribbean immigrants in the United States, Caribbean people have consciously developed perceptions about race and ethnicity that influences their self-concept and identification. These perceptions also inform their decisions regarding the kinds of associations they join, the neighborhoods they reside in, and the jobs they seek (Kasinitz 1992; Stepick, Rey, and Mahler 2009; Vickerman 1999; Waters 1999). The xenophobia and institutional racism Caribbean immigrants "have encountered upon their arrival in the United States has played a large part in the evolution of a complex and, at times, contradictory awareness of their ethnicity," Black master status, and in their grasp of the dynamics of American race relations (Ho 1991). For example, some Caribbean immigrants may view being American as something positive because such an identity symbolizes certain power, while on the other hand, other Caribbean immigrants may perceive being American as being stigmatized and labeled as African American—a group that has a low social status in American society (Foner 1987; Kasinitz 1992; Rong, Lang, and Fitchett 2008; Vickerman 1994). Hence, when scholars (Portes 1995; Portes and Zhou 1993; Rumbaut 1994; Waters 1999) focus on race as an important factor that determines ethnic identity assertions of Caribbean immigrants, they find that there are certain advantages (social and economic) and perceived cultural worth to identifying as a Caribbean immigrant (Berry and Phinney 2006). Thus, in response to America's racist assumptions regarding individuals of African ancestry, Caribbean immigrants may internalize these perceived advantages and consciously choose to utilize a wider range of ethnic identity options to set them apart from other racial and immigrant groups.

To understand the social and economic circumstances that influence Caribbean immigrant adaptation, acculturation, and ultimately their ethnic identity assertions it is also critical to examine the ways host communities, governments, and social systems influence patterns of assimilation. Studies to date utilize Portes and Rumbaut's (2001, 2003) influential segmented assimilation theory as a means to explain variations in immigration and acculturation within the context of family systems or schools. Scholars agree community and family ties not only provide social networks and financial assistance are essential to the acculturation process. Also, the acculturation process depends on ethnic immigrant enclave capacities and social networks (Alba and Nee 2003; Benson 2006; Kivisto 2005; Levitt and Jaworksy 2007; Rong, Lang and Fitchett 2008). This is true particularly for Caribbean immigrants who experience racial isolation from mainstream American society due to their Black master status. Community-based organizations serve as a primary resource for Caribbean immigrants and their families learning to navigate through race-based systems of bureaucracy once they arrive in America.

Community-based organizations are the sites for the transmission of laws, rules, cultural beliefs, and ideologies where individuals share information and expand social networks. As a critical socializing context for social networks and families, community-based organizations can determine the extent to which ethnic immigrants, and particularly Black Caribbean immigrants, can develop positive self concepts and ethnic identification. In areas with well functioning Black Caribbean immigrant communities, the strength of social networks, family, and organizational affiliations can reinforce the cultural ideology regarding the importance of race and ethnic identity. In this regard, such organizations can provide the resources to support immigrants' resistance to adversarial subcultures and promote the creation and assertion of ethnic identity options. Yet, despite the attention given to the immigrant experiences of Black Caribbean immigrants, few studies have examined the specific role community-based social service organizations play in the development and assertion of their immigrant ethnic identity options and segmented assimilation once they arrive in the America.

The research presented here intends to advance the scholarship on Caribbean immigrant acculturation by focusing on the specific role and functions community-based organizations play in facilitating the creation of Black ethnic identity options for Caribbean immigrants. This case study uses 29 in-depth semi-structured interviews with staff, and affiliated members (i.e., community members/social activists, political leaders) of a grassroots, community-based organization, called The Caribbean Service Center. Located in an area many consider the Caribbean Mecca of New York City – central Brooklyn, The Caribbean Service Center's thirty year-old history, external and internal policies, and relationship with a large racial and ethnic immigrant community serves as an ideal site to explore how a community-based organization can promote and support various Caribbean ethnic identity options and influence immigrant acculturation.

In particular, this case study examines three critical issues concerning the role of organizations and its influence on immigrant acculturation: (1) the internal socio-organizational conditions that influence the ethnic identity assertion and maintenance of varied Caribbean ethnic identities, (2) the function of The Caribbean Service Center-- its history, structure, and client-staff interactions, and activities (e.g., provision of health and social services to Caribbeans, building Caribbean community resources or social capital, and maintaining ties to Caribbean communities in the United States and the Caribbean), and (3) the unique racial, social and political circumstances posed by the political environment (e.g., federal and state immigration policies) that effect how The Caribbean Service Center advocates on behalf of the Caribbean immigrant community as well as the broader Black community, and how Caribbean immigrants understand their racial status (as Black people) in American society.

At first glance, the research presented highlights an organization whose history, staffing, and community population is largely Caribbean-identified. The research suggests that through The Caribbean Service Center, racial and ethnic distinctions that exist between Caribbeans and African Americans are emphasized, and maintained in order for positive ethnic identity options to persist. Upon deeper exploration, the research reveals that while The Caribbean Service Center creates a necessary opportunity for Caribbean immigrants to interpret the meanings of race and discrimination and its determining power in affecting their ability to improve their life chances, The Caribbean Service Center's practices, culture, and ideology also creates tension within the broader Black community. This case study does take into account the fact that many Caribbean immigrants are exposed to and learn the meanings behind racial-ethnic identities (i.e., what it means to be African American versus Caribbean and race ideologies through the media, family, and their social networks prior to their arrival in the United States (see Waters 1999:38). Yet, when Caribbean immigrants arrive in the United States and become clients in organizations, it is within this context that Caribbean immigrants learn under which circumstances they should consider themselves primarily as African American, as immigrants, or as both. It is at this point, I suggest, Caribbean immigrants' understandings about race prior to migrating to the United States goes from being fairly abstract to being more experiential and more consciously life-shaping (see Vickerman 1999). The process by which community-based organizations facilitate Caribbean immigrants' creation and maintenance of Black ethnic identity options also has the potential to reify racial ideologies that denigrate those who have low racial status-- American-born Blacks. Ultimately, the reification of such racial ideologies, over time, will prove to be detrimental to all racial-ethnic immigrants who share phenotypic characteristics with African Americans.

Drawing on sociological literature that addresses race, immigration, ethnic identity, and social organizations, the research presented examines the organizational circumstances in which Caribbean immigrants learn what ethnic identity options are available to them, whether these identity options are supported or denigrated by The Caribbean Service Center and its staff, and how these identities are maintained over time. To understand Caribbean immigrants and their acculturation process, the research utilizes theories of immigrant incorporation and the social construction of race, political economy, and human relations to explore how the intersection of skin color, immigrant status, and organizational influence shape ethnic identities options that Caribbean immigrants assert.

Situating the Research: Sociological Theoretical Orientations on Race, Ethnicity, Immigration, and Organizations

For over 45 years, researchers have either countered or elaborated on earlier views of assimilation and immigrant acculturation. In the early 1920s, race and immigration scholars used assimilation theory to highlight the process of assimilation, ethnic identity construction, social achievement and assimilation of immigrants, and discern whether immigrants can fully assimilate in accordance to an American ethos. At the time, proponents (Park and Burgess 1924; Warner and Srole, 1945; Park 1950; Gordon 1964) defined assimilation as the "process of interpenetration and fusion in which persons and groups acquire the memories, sentiments, and attitudes of the dominant group and by sharing their experience and history are incorporated with them in a common cultural life" (see Park and Burgess 1924: 735). Robert E. Park developed a progressive and irreversible four-stage "race relations cycle (contact, competition, accommodation, and finally, assimilation) to suggest that immigrants over time will undergo a linear process whereby they become more "Americanized" by unlearning their "inferior" cultural traits to "successfully learn the new way of life necessary for full acceptance" (see also Warner and Srole 1945).

Through the mid-1960s, others as Milton Gordon's (1964) *Assimilation in American Life* elaborated on Park's construct of assimilation into a conceptual framework. In his paradigm, Gordon described seven dimensions of assimilation (cultural, marital, identification, attitude-receptional, behavior-receptional, civic, and structural assimilation). Gordon's dimension of structural assimilation, in particular, is critical to understanding the process by which immigrants acculturate and later experience upward and downward mobility. Structural assimilation occurs when the host group admits immigrants into their organizations and allows immigrants to become a part of the host group's social networks. Immigrants' penetration of the host group's organizations and social networks allows immigrants to become a part of a common cultural life. Therefore, immigrants accept and internalize the values and culture of the host group-- including the meanings of race and ethnic identity.

Together, scholars Park and Gordon argued that assimilation and acculturation requires the acquisition of cultural characteristics of American society and the participation of the entire society, including the immigrant population. Their paradigms assume that the greater congruence between American citizens and the immigrant population, the less likely conflict will exist. This point is critical to the analysis of classic assimilation theory because it reveals that assimilation is very much dependent on the view American society has of the immigrant population and how well American society, with the use of power and resources, can easily mesh immigrants into its general population.

Up to this point, much of the literature did not fully explore the paradox of American society with regard to race, racial classification, and immigrant status for people of color (Stone 1985). Interesting as it is ironic, immigration and race is and has always been at the very core of American sociological research, but unfortunately much of that literature only focused on European immigrants and their acculturation experience. It is for this same reason that today's scholars, such as Glazer (1993: 122), view assimilation as an "ideologically laden residue of worn-out sociological theories" and as an "ethnocentric and patronizing imposition on minority people struggling to retain their cultural and ethnic integrity" (see Massey 1994: 21). These scholars suggest that while Black immigrants share many characteristics with Irish, Italian, and Jewish immigrants that preceded them (e.g., work ethic, fervent religious commitment, and a strong emphasis on family and education), they are not white immigrants but immigrants of color.

A common argument against the assimilation model-- the absorption of one culture into the dominant culture-- is that assimilation is less available to racial and ethnic immigrants because of their non-European origins. As Laguerre (1984) suggests, the racial barrier adds a dimension to the everyday problems newcomers face; skin color becomes a problem, by undercutting assimilation, and one that cannot be overcome. In the Caribbean for example, the social meaning of race is influenced by color and class distinctions, whether light/dark-skinned and rich/poor. In contrast, the social meaning of race is more rigid in the United States. The Caribbean immigrant is seen first as a Black person and being Black makes assimilation less possible. In this regard, the process of assimilation is not so much one of willingness to be assimilated on the part of the immigrant, as it is one of acceptance by American society (Van den Berghe 1981). Hence, scholars' conceptions of assimilation as "inevitable" in multiethnic societies cannot be used to examine the diverse experiences of post-1965 racial-ethnic immigrants.

To counter the increasing dissent amongst today's scholars regarding applicability of the assimilation framework for racial-ethnic immigrants, Kazal (1995), Morawska (1994), and Alba and Nee (1995, 1997) maintain that "whatever the deficiencies of earlier formulations and application, this social science concept [assimilation] offers the best way to understand and describe the integration into mainstream experiences across generation...even if it cannot be regarded as a universal outcome of American life" (see Alba and Nee 1997: 827). Instead, scholars Alba and Nee (2005) define assimilation not as a linear process of ethnic obliteration but a dynamic one in which minority and majority cultures influence one another. In their research, Alba and Nee (2005) use an assimilation framework to understand the ways immigrants from Asia, Africa, Latin America, and the Caribbean are likely to change America at least as much as America changes them.

An alternate framework to understanding the experiences of racial-ethnic immigrants is segmented assimilation. Segmented assimilation posits a more fluid and reflexive relationship between immigrants and American society by contending that racial identities are not fixed but are social constructions "produced through the interaction of societal systems of racial classification and human agency" (see Benson, 2006: 222; also Cornell and Hartmann 1998; Omi and Winant 1994). Immigrant incorporation can occur along multiple paths, with different segments of the population, and at varying rates, depending both on the characteristics of the immigrant group and how the group is received in American society (Benson 2006; Duany 1998; Vickerman 1994, 1999).

According to Benson (2006: 222), segmented assimilation suggests that "Black migrants will not be uniformly incorporated; [instead] there will be variation in the way Black migrant groups construct their racial identities in the U.S. society." One explanation for the diversity in migrant incorporation experiences is the construction and the assertion of a distinct racial and ethnic identity. Evidence suggests that the process, albeit the rate of Caribbean immigrant segmented assimilation is facilitated by community-based organizations (see the works of Kasinitz 1992; Rogers 2004). Specifically, scholars (Basch 1987; Lissak 1989; Massey 1987) have emphasized that the adaptation, incorporation, and the maintenance of Caribbean immigrants' ethnic identities are strongly related to the organizations that serve them.

Community-based organizations that serve Caribbean immigrants have a central role in teaching and promoting certain racial and cultural ideals, norms, and values about culture, race, and identity in the United States (Basch 1987; Kasinitz 1992). Organizations set the frames for human interaction, both within the organization and the larger society. Individuals apply the organization's value system to their lives (Ahrne 1993; Aldrich 1999; Minkoff 1995). It is within these institutional and community contexts or social circumstances that many Caribbean immigrants learn which racial and ethnic identity will better assist them to achieve goals of success. Vickerman (1999:168) argues that Caribbean immigrants learn that there are three possible ethnic options that exist: "(1) adopt the identity of Black (i.e., in the sense of the term which involves the traditional, unflattering stereotypes--lazy, untrustworthy, and illiterate); (2) establish a West Indian/Caribbean, immigrant identity; or (3) identify with African Americans on some issues, such as discrimination and inequality, but distance from them (i.e., emphasizing their 'West Indian-ness') on others." Based on their interaction with and treatment by staff workers within an organization, Caribbean immigrants face the task of establishing and utilizing one of these identity options through the use of language, choice of dress, and public affiliation in order to gain access to certain material, social, or political opportunities open to them in America (Bryce-Laporte 1972; Ringer and Lawless 1989; Waters 1999).

Understanding the exchange relationship between immigrants of color and organizational practices is also critical to grasping the negotiation and maintenance of ethnic identity. It is within this exchange that determines the rate by which clients learn and internalize the norms and values of American society (March and Simon 1958). The structured, patterned relationship or interchange between organizations, their clients, and the social environment allows for the exchange of information-- of norms and values to take place (Abrams 1975; Burns and Stalker 1994; Igelhard and Becerra 1995; Kast and Rosenzweig 1973; Lawrence and Lorsch 1967; Parsons 1937). Scholars suggest that the exchange of information that takes place between an organization and its social environment (e.g., federal and state policies, racial and economic politics, and demographic shifts) impacts an organization's function, goals, and ability to socialize and meet the needs and demands of its clients (Igelhard and Becerra 1995).

Qualitative studies on immigrant associations at the turn of the twentieth century focused on how the church developed intricate social welfare systems in response to the needs of immigrants and the effects these systems had on immigrants' assimilation and socioeconomic mobility. Research by Litt (1970), Kim (1991, 1994), and Kwon (1997) focused on the influence religious participation had on political integration, whereas Dolan (1975) and Gleason (1968) emphasized how these associations helped immigrants to retain their cultural heritage in their host country (also see studies by Brown 1991; Menjívar 1999; Nelli 1970; Levitt 1998; Orsi 1985; Warner 1993; Warner and Wittner 1998). More recently, because of the ever-increasing racial, ethnic, linguistic, and cultural heterogeneity of these immigrants, scholars reframed their research questions to emphasize race and racial discrimination and whether social institutions impede or facilitate immigrant incorporation into the host society. Jenkins (1988) explored the role ethnicity played in social service provisions and how the social service provision industry had to adapt to changing and diverse populations. Basch (1987) examined voluntary associations among Vincentian and Grenadian Caribbean immigrants and found that these immigrant associations provided direct assistance to co-ethnics as well as other Caribbeans in the community, the boroughs of Queens and Brooklyn, and city-wide. Kasinitz (1992:111-123) also discussed the role that community-based organizations played in the mobilization, political representation, and incorporation of Caribbeans in New York City (also see Rogers 2004).

In spite of scholars' prolific writings, little is understood about these organizations, the programs and services they provide, their ideology, culture, and climate, and the kinds of resources (e.g., information, and networks with clients) they use to help their immigrant clients create and sustain strong Caribbean ethnic identities options. Utilizing segmented assimilation, political economy, and human relations frameworks, this case study shows the somewhat contradictory process that The Caribbean Service Center strives to assist in the adaptation and acculturation of its Caribbean clients into American culture. Employing segmented assimilation, this research argues that The Caribbean Service Center slows the rate of their immigrant incorporation by helping them to retain the traditions and norms of the Caribbean region, and maintain Caribbean ethnic identities (also see Basch 1992).

This case study also utilizes political economy and human relations to point to the interpersonal influence and social power The Caribbean Service Center and its staff members has on their immigrant clients' attitudes and perceptions regarding the dynamics of race and ethnic relations. Specifically, a political-economy framework draws attention to the internal and external political power and economic system, which determine and influence what The Caribbean Service Center does to serve its diverse client population (see Zald 1970; Wamsley and Zald 1973). The research presented shows how The Caribbean Service Center's external polities (e.g., federal and state funding opportunities) affect its mission, aims, and goals, as well as serves to reaffirm and sanction its existence and role within the community and the larger social environment. The case study also focuses on The Caribbean Service Center's internal polity (i.e., staff attitudes and values) and its direct impact on The Caribbean Service Center's activities, programs, ability to support their clients and deliver services (Igelhard and Becerra 1995). To further explore The Caribbean Service Center's internal polity, a human relations framework is employed to examine how its staff receives clients and their presenting problems, identify with their clients' experiences, and interact with other staff and community members (see Heesacker and Carroll 1997; McGregor 1960; Schneider, Brief, and Guzzo 1996). This case study argues that staff members' internalization of The Caribbean Service Center's ideology, culture, and climate impact staff engagement and interaction with clients, and influence staff efforts in shaping its immigrant client attitudes, perceptions, and/or behaviors, including ethnic identity option.

Description of Research: *Significance of Place-- Why Brooklyn?*

New York City continues to serve as a port of entry for millions of immigrants from all corners of the world, each bringing a breadth of racial, cultural, linguistic, and religious diversity to the United States. The long history of Caribbean migration to New York City and the prominent size of today's Caribbean and Caribbean American communities, in particular, make the Caribbean immigrant experience in New York and in Brooklyn, significant (Foner 1987, 2001). With its deep, rich history filled with both camaraderie and tension between and within ethnic groups, the research setting of Brooklyn, New York for this case study speaks to the acculturation experiences Caribbeans have had in the city since they first arrived that ultimately shape their outlook on life in America.

Historically, New York City's harbor, including Brooklyn's maritime industry, played a significant role in establishing New York City as an immigrant epicenter. In the 1830s, the City's harbor served as means of possible continued economic enterprise and entrepreneurship for white immigrants whose livelihoods in their homelands depended on cargo or shipping. For today's immigrants, including Caribbean immigrants, advances in technology and education makes the possibilities of entrepreneurship in New York City a very attractive place to live (Bretell 2000).

At the height of America's immigration boom of the 1850s and with the start of construction of the Brooklyn Bridge in 1883, Brooklyn's residential population grew from 15,400 to approximately 97,000, with over 75% being either Irish or German immigrants. By the end of the 19th century, Brooklyn was not only primarily inhabited by immigrants but also ranked the seventh largest, wealthiest, and heavily populated city in the United States (Foster, 1967). In 1900, with completion of the Brooklyn Bridge and the annexation of Brooklyn to New York, the population of Brooklyn grew to 1,166,582. The Bridge and the invention of highways and automobiles created possibilities for more travel between Brooklyn and Manhattan. People, particularly European immigrants, were able to travel and migrate throughout these two boroughs of New York City. Brooklyn's quickly diminishing rural/farm land in its most central area developed to house brownstones and tree-lined streets with colonial style homes--made this borough an ideal representation of "the sanctity of suburbia, minutes from City life" (Caro 1974). With its beautiful landscaping and country appeal, location near Prospect Park and Gardens, its availability of housing, and opportunity to purchase large homes--all of which gave Brooklyn an appeal for those who were upwardly mobile and who desired an affluent lifestyle (Caro 1974).

Like European immigrants, Caribbean immigrants also found New York City, particularly Brooklyn, an ideal and beautiful place to live. Between 1900 and 1930, Caribbean migration to the United States was not as numerically substantial as European immigration, but was very significant to the social and demographic landscape of the time. According to Handlin (1959: 48-49) Caribbean migration to the United

States reached to 40,000 by 1910; of these one-quarter settled in New York City. Between 1910 and the late1940s, Caribbean migration grew to over 50,000, significantly impacting the number of Blacks living in New York City. During this time, New York City was the only city in the United States where a substantial proportion of the Black population was of Caribbean origin (Kasinitz 1992). Prior to settling in Brooklyn, many Caribbeans migrated to and formed communities in upper Manhattan and Harlem where native-born Blacks also resided. Caribbean immigrants were influential in these communities, in establishing businesses and contributing to the flourishing intellectual, political, and artistic base during the Harlem Renaissance in the 1920s.

Between the 1930s and the post-World War II era, the National Origins Act and the McCarran-Walter Act of 1952 restricted the flow of immigrants based on their place of origin, and forced immigration to the United States to decline sharply. Caribbeans in New York City felt the impact of these immigration policies on already strained race and ethnic relations in the City between Blacks and whites as well as between Caribbeans and African Americans. Glazer and Moynihan (1963:28) suggest that this was a period of limited jobs and resources for all citizens, and particularly racial-ethnic citizens who were dependent on casual labor and household services as a means of employment, and suffered far more than any other group living in any part of the city. This economic suffering and competition caused much strife between Black ethnics. New York's continual city-wide migration allowed many to look to Brooklyn for employment and other means of economic survival. With increasing city-wide migration, city planners decided to build subways from Manhattan to central Brooklyn. The planners believed that the City's first train connection, the "A-train," a subway system connecting Harlem, Manhattan to Bedford-Stuyvesant, Brooklyn would increase real estate ownership and provide greater opportunity for domestic-related employment in this part of the City.

With employment constraints and competition between Caribbean immigrants and African Americans, many Caribbean immigrants learned from other Caribbeans (e.g., immigrants and Caribbean associations) that they must maintain an ethnic identity separate from the African American population in order to increase their employment opportunities. The maintenance of ethnic identity separation can be attributed to the fact that Caribbeans were seen as generally snobbish and status conscious and often looked down upon working class and poorer African Americans for their lack of education and proper work ethic (Bryce-Laporte 1972; Klevan 1990). According to Bryce-Laporte (1972), many Caribbeans were considered by whites to be ambitious, to have fine-tuned skills, willing to learn new trades and professions, and hard working and focused on shedding traditional agrarian skills for those required of urban life. Thus, many Caribbeans saw migrating to Brooklyn as another way to separate themselves from African Americans. By moving to Brooklyn, Caribbean immigrants established themselves as different from African Americans by forming Caribbean ethnic enclaves and social organizations to promote their distinctiveness.

Prior to Caribbean migration to Brooklyn, Brooklyn was seen as a potpourri of white ethnic communities: Jewish, Italian, German, Scandinavian, and Slavic. However, with economic and immigration shifts, the presence of a significant Black (immigrant and American-born) community began to emerge. Caribbean immigrants and some African Americans, who could afford to move from Harlem to central Brooklyn, migrated for the same reasons white ethnics moved to Brooklyn--the middle class dream. Between the 1940s and the 1950s, the Black population in Brooklyn grew from approximately 7 percent to 33 percent. Although over 70 percent of some of Brooklyn's neighborhoods were still predominately white, these neighborhoods no longer constituted an exclusive white community that existed just two and a half decades earlier of "old" new Americans. Caribbean migrants settled in central areas of Brooklyn such as Bedford-Stuyvesant, Crown Heights, Flatbush and East Flatbush, which are inland-sections of Brooklyn, all near the "A" train and far from the textile factories that were prevalent in the downtown area of the borough.

Caribbean immigrants who arrived in New York after the Immigration Act of 1965 relied on networks to find employment, housing, and other opportunities established by earlier Caribbean migrants. For many of these Caribbean immigrants, Brooklyn became the heart of their survival; it is "the home away from home" that draws many to vibrant Caribbean community and institutions, including sources of information about life in the United States. Today, central Brooklyn--Bedford-Stuyvesant, Crown Heights, and Flatbush neighborhoods--continues to have the largest concentration of Caribbean immigrants in New York City. By the mid-1980s, the

number of Caribbean immigrants in Brooklyn alone increased to
133,000, compared to the City's overall immigrant growth of 150,000
Anglophone Caribbean immigrants. Between 1990 and 2000, the
numbers of Caribbeans living in Brooklyn and in New York City is
significant, considering that the United States' overall Caribbean
immigration population at the time was 328,000 and represented
approximately 4% of the Black population in the country (INS Bureau
and New York City Planning Commission; Williams et al 2007). In
2000, the total foreign-born population of New York City grew to 2.9
million, with Brooklyn having approximately 932,000 foreign-born
residents. Those who are Anglophone Caribbean immigrants
comprised one-third of foreign-born residents (see Appendix A, Table
1 and Figures 2-5). Today, Caribbean immigrants to New York City
and to the borough of Brooklyn continue to grow steadily by 86,000
each year (INS Bureau and New York City Planning Commission).

Description of Research: *Significance of Space*

With the growing presence of a diverse ethnic and Caribbean
immigrant population in Brooklyn, immigration and acculturation of
these "new" Americans continues to be a mainstay of public concern.
At the forefront of public discourse are several questions that point to
how these immigrants fare: What is their acculturation experience like
as it relates to inclusion and exclusion, community development and
disenfranchisement, and government responsibility? How does the
acculturation experience impact immigrants' self concept and outlook
on life in their new country? Because this case study examines the role
community-based organizations play in influencing how Caribbean
immigrants think about race, ethnicity, and identity, it was critical to
identify a community-based organization that was established during
the height of major demographic change, which resulted from 1960s
immigration policies, and persists today. In particular, a receptive
social and political climate toward immigrants as well as a well
organized and sustainable advocacy network is essential for
community-based services for ethnic immigrants to advance over time.
Second, it was important to identify a community-based organization
that is a provider of human and social services with a commitment to
serving racial-ethnic and Caribbean immigrant community members,

supporting and empowering their families, encouraging local businesses, and being sensitive to their cultural and immigrant needs. While there are several organizations in central Brooklyn that were established post-1965 and provide a myriad of social services to racial-ethnic, immigrant populations, many of these organizations diverged in their capacity and resources to provide services for more than 150 neighborhoods in central Brooklyn alone. Also, some of the differences between these organizations were based on whether they were categorized as immigrant and/or ethnic-based. There are two elements that determine whether an organization can be categorized as immigrant and/or ethnic-based. First, the organization's executive Board and founders must represent to the staff, clients, and other members outside of the organization that they are committed to ethnic and immigrant populations. Second, the ethnic background of the staff is central to the work and culture of the organization and whether clients and the community at large identify with the organization and its staff ethnicity. Several community-based organizations in central Brooklyn work predominantly with clients from a cluster of countries, in Asia, Latin America, the Caribbean, and Europe, to avoid being barred from receiving public funding for discriminating on the basis of national origin. In these cases, such organizations had small numbers of Caribbean clients. In a few instances, there were organizations that were not community-based at all, but sizable programs affiliated with large corporations in the community.

The Caribbean Service Center, on the other hand, is a community-based organization and provider of services to racial-ethnics, with a particular focus on Caribbean immigrant and Black ethnic communities. The Caribbean Service Center concentrates its efforts in central Brooklyn while also offering services throughout the entire metropolitan area. The Caribbean Service Center is different from many other organizations in the community for the following reasons: first, it is incorporated as a nonprofit organization; second, The Caribbean Service Center has paid professional full-time and part-time staff, offices open to the public with regular service hours, and some sources of funding; third, it offers a broad range of health and social services to immigrants from the Caribbean and Black ethnic groups in many racial-ethnic neighborhoods in the City; fourth, in addition to providing these services, The Caribbean Service Center is also concerned with promoting social, economic, and immigrant ties, connections and activities between Caribbean immigrants in New York and their countries of origin. Many of its activities are focused on community events that help connect immigrants to the issues of their home countries. Finally, The Caribbean Service Center was cited as one of New York City's leading nonprofit entities that provide cultural and social services to racial-ethnic, immigrants, therefore, giving it legitimacy in the community and the city as a whole. Taking these factors into consideration, The Caribbean Service Center was selected as an ideal site for this case study.

Description of Research: *Sampling of Respondents*

The research presented in this case study is based on semi-structured interviews with a total of 29 individuals affiliated with The Caribbean Service Center (nine Board members, executive director, Founder, eight staff members, and ten community leaders) in central Brooklyn's Caribbean community. Nearly nine months of qualitative data collection (i.e., participant-observation, interviews, and archival data collection) commenced in late March and concluded in early December 2004. A list of semi-structured and open-ended questions was developed to probe the perceptions participants of the organization's program and structural levels and affiliates, including its Founder, the director, the program managers, and community leaders about workplace relationships, staff-client interactions, and community issues and challenges. In addition, this case study also draws upon limited ethnographic observations made in community sites--watching, listening, and passing time with Caribbean immigrants, some clients of the organizations and other community members.

Participants ranged in age-- from mid-to-late 20s to early 60s. Except for two participants, fourteen participants are first-generation immigrants (born abroad and immigrated as an adult) while thirteen participants are 1.5 generation (born abroad and immigrated as a child). These participants came to the United States between the early 1970s and mid 1980s. They were a mix of quasi-, semi-, and professionals, with their highest education degrees ranging from a high school diploma to some graduate school to a doctoral degree. Specifically, three staff members had a high school diploma with at least two years of college course work completed; six participants (two staff members and four community leaders) had Bachelor degrees while nine participants (Founder, two staff members, two Board members, and four community leaders) had Master's degrees and additional certification in areas of social work, journalism, public administration, sociology, psychology, and human services. Finally, eleven participants (one staff member, the executive director, two community leaders, and seven Board members) had doctorates in areas of sociology, social work, psychology, environmental science, and law. The sample of participants also was mixed in terms of social class. Most participants perceived themselves as middle- and upper middle class with only three staff members identifying themselves as working class. In many regards, participants held subjective definitions of specific class labels (i.e., middle class) by identifying with factors that determine such identities (e.g., economic position, degree of job security, education, social status). Participants also differed in the meanings and perceptions of these factors and its impact on daily life. It is important to note that the extent to which these participants define and perceive social class influences their segmented assimilation paths, including ethnic identity assertions. Typically, social scientists have argued, middle class Black immigrants are more likely to live in residential isolation of the suburbs, far from traditional domestic Black residential concentrations of the inner city. As a result, scholars have suggested that middle class Black immigrants are more likely to assert specific ethnic and national identities as opposed to working class Black immigrants who tend to live amongst and receive similar treatment as native-born Blacks (see Rong, Lang, and Fitchett 2008). Interestingly, within the community context of central Brooklyn, with its distinct middle class enclaves bleeding into working class areas, the "melting pot" experience of New York inner city life meshes the experience of Caribbean Black immigrants of all social classes. Hence, the class consciousness of this study's participants really points to the existence of a more fluid and complex variation of meanings and occupational and economic images immigrants bring with them from their home countries and use for different purposes and strategies in America.

In terms of nationality, an overwhelming majority of participants were Panamanian, but also present were Jamaicans, Trinidadians, Grenadians, Haitians, Barbadians (Bajans), Monserratians, Anguillians, St. Lucians, and Dominicans. This diverse representation of participants speaks, in an interesting way, to the intra-ethnic, cultural, and linguistic diversity of Caribbean community members that work with and receive services from The Caribbean Service Center. Finally, all but three participants are United States' citizens. A list of participants, along with information about their age, education, ethnic identification options is presented in the Appendix. Their names and all other identifying characteristics have been changed.

A Few Points to Consider

I have a personal interest in understanding how community-based organizations influence the negotiation and maintenance of ethnic identities. I grew up in Brooklyn, New York, in the 1980s and '90s. As a child of Caribbean immigrants who came to America in the early 1970s, I learned to identify with my parents' culture by eating Caribbean food, speaking patois, singing and dancing to calypso, soca, and reggae, and traveling to and from the islands. The Brooklyn communities of Flatbush, Park Slope, and Eastern Parkway, where we lived with other foreign-born or 1.5 generation Caribbean immigrants, also made identifying with my Caribbean heritage easy. It was not until the early 1990s, following the Crown Heights Riot and its aftermath and while attending a predominately white private high school, that I became more conscious about race, ethnicity, and class. I began to realize the pervasive and insidious nature of race that often plagued my own and my family members' lives.

My parents and I would share stories of our experiences at work, school, and retold stories of other family members' experiences in dealing with prejudice and discrimination in New York City. Many of our experiences with race, ethnicity, and discrimination were often within institutional settings. As a result, I became aware of the role institutions played in shaping my and my parents' perceptions about the importance of race and ethnicity. Within these institutional settings, I learned the costs and benefits of what it means to be Black, immigrant, and Caribbean in America. Such lessons inevitably shaped my own understanding of race and ethnic identity and the circumstances under which I negotiate my racial and ethnic identity and options to assert a Caribbean immigrant-identified ethnic identity or a Black racial identity. These lessons provoked me to explore further the process of negotiating ethnic identities and how Caribbean people come to understand the politics of race and Black identity within organizations and choose to maintain ethnic distinctiveness as Caribbeans.

Throughout this book the term "Caribbean" is used to refer to individuals with ancestry in countries bordering the Caribbean sea (Costa Rica, Honduras, Panama, Columbia, Belize, Guyana), within territories of the Greater Antilles (e.g., Puerto Rico, Haiti, Cuba and Jamaica), and the Lesser Antilles (e.g., Martinique, St. Lucia, Anguilla, St. Vincent, Grenada, Barbados, Antigua, Montserrat, St. Kitts, the Virgin Islands, Trinidad and Tobago) who share similar foods, music, lifestyle, and a common historical background. The term Caribbean, however, is not accepted by all groups, with some individuals preferring to be referred to as "West Indian." By some, the designation of West Indian is used interchangeably with Caribbean but often refers to those with ancestry from territories relating to the Lesser Antilles or the British Caribbean.

Interestingly, the term West Indian is rejected by others who consider it to be an insulting term that refers to Christopher Columbus' ignorance as to the geographic location of the Caribbean and its location being west of India. On the other hand, the term Caribbean has been strongly criticized due to the fact it combines people coming from different countries with different histories. Such labeling puts together people from different classes and races and mixes people with various histories of oppression (see Gimenez 1992; Massey 1993). These critiques are appropriate as the Caribbean population is indeed extremely heterogeneous—ethnically, racially, linguistically, and socio-economically. The fact still remains, however, that "the constant use by different social actors of these [two terms] can sometimes give rise in reality, by the specific effectiveness of evocation, to the very thing they represent" (Bourdieu 1991:222; see also Itzigsohn and Dore-Cabral 2000). While the term Caribbean can be deemed as controversial, many of the individuals who participated in this research, identified with the term Caribbean. Hence, the term Caribbean is employed to indicate the common background of custom, geography, language, and the immigrant experience.

This case study profiles The Caribbean Service Center, its staff and affiliated members' accounts of their personal and cultural beliefs, sense of identity, personal settlement history and paths of acculturation, The Caribbean Service Center's role in creating ethnic identity options for its Black Caribbean immigrants, and the challenges and concerns the Caribbean and broader Black community face as a result of these ethnic identity options. Hence, this book is not neutral; it is motivated by the notion that it is critical to explore the complexities, including the social cost and benefits, of Caribbean ethnic and racial identity formations and what this means for Black identity within individual, institutional and socio-political contexts. The research points to the ways ethnic identity formations feed into the American construction of ethnic "others" that, in contradictory ways, empower Black immigrants but also perpetuate racial-ethnic tensions between African Americans and Caribbeans.

CHAPTER 2

From Grassroots Movement to
Rise of an Organization

*One's background shapes his or her attitude, perception and
perspective. So, having knowledge of a Caribbean background
or culture is a requirement for serving people from the
Caribbean.*

(Archibald Dubnet, Board member)

Like the native-born African American population, America's
immigrants of color seek solace and desire equitable treatment in this
country. Community members and social service providers who work
closely with racial-ethnic immigrants realize that language, culture, and
race and ethnicity are factors that contribute to the poverty and
discrimination these immigrants experience. In many ways, social
service providers are responsible for addressing such needs in ways that
respect racial-ethnics' diversity and differences. Providers address
these concerns by developing programs and services in community-
based organizations. Providers have developed and participated in
organizations such as the Urban League (UL) and the Negro Young
Men's Christian Association (Negro YMCA) in Brooklyn, New York,
dating as far back as the early twentieth century. At the time, these
organizations focused on minimizing ghettoization in central Brooklyn
by (1) investigating Black housing conditions, racial separation,
discrimination, and paternalism; (2) organizing church meetings; and
(3) providing assistance to Black families and children.

By the late 1960s and 1970s, with the passing of the Immigration and Naturalization Act of 1965, service providers and community members found that such organizations' programming and services were unable to handle the diverse needs of a growing Caribbean immigrant population in central Brooklyn. As a result, new types of organizations--grassroots and action based--grew up and became complementary to older organizations in the existing organizational structure and community.

These emerging organizations offered racial-ethnics a welcomed help for an array of social problems that they had often been forced to handle themselves without support. Many of these programs offered services that were locally based in the community--outpatient, inexpensive, convenient, and more tolerant of racial-ethnics and immigrants than the other alternatives. Providers involved volunteers, community members, and especially clients in the design and implementation of programming with the understanding that services and resources would be available to anyone in their target community who wanted and needed it. In many regards, these programs illustrate how community-based providers must understand their clients' inner lives in order to better serve them and meet their needs. The development and establishment of The Caribbean Services Center offers a similar and notably remarkable snapshot of this process. Identifying a larger community need for improving the well-being of Caribbean immigrants was a major part of the approach providers took to better serve the needs of recent Caribbean immigrants. Despite their varied experiences in delivering services to diverse Black ethnics in New York City, particularly Brooklyn, providers' shared perspective laid the basis for a movement to form, a community of people who not only could share their ideas and feelings about improving and empowering Caribbean immigrants and their families in need, but also each other. One of these new organizations was The Caribbean Service Center.

This chapter explores the history of the founding of The Caribbean Service Center and its transformation from a grassroots movement to a community-based organization. I consider how a group of Caribbean immigrant nursing students saw the needs and concerns of a growing Black, immigrant population in the densely populated central Brooklyn community and, in effect, gave birth to a movement and organization that addresses social and health issues among racial-ethnic, Caribbean immigrant groups. My approach here looks specifically at The Caribbean Service Center's grassroots history as being critical to its organizational ideology, community rapport, and Caribbean identity consciousness. My purpose here is not to detail all aspects of the founding in its entirety but to demonstrate how The Caribbean Service Center's grassroots and organizational beginnings shows its continual support of Caribbean immigrants, their culture, and ultimately their Caribbean ethnic identity. Briefly discussing the collective action of a small group of service providers, which served as the impetus for the founding of The Caribbean Service Center, is more about the conditions under which community providers of Caribbean descent become involved in activism and the social and cultural context that goaded them to establish Caribbean-focused community interventions. These conditions include the structures and processes in place to help mobilize, the providers' existing social ties to community leadership, and their perceptions of hope for the future and collective efficacy to improve the lives of new racial-ethnic immigrants (see Foster-Fishman, Cantillon, and Van Egeren 2007).

Central Brooklyn's Socio-demographic Profile-1970s to 1980s

The socio-demographic portrait of the central Brooklyn community during the 1970s and early 1980s is critical to understanding the community context in which The Caribbean Service Center was developed. This portrait describes the immigrant population at the time (e.g., their age, gender, native origin and occupational background) and gives insight into how community organizers identified the challenges these recent Caribbean immigrants faced.

Caribbeans comprised a major portion of immigrants coming to New York City in the post-1965 era. Caribbean immigrants constituted approximately thirty-seven percent of all immigrants in the 1970s and forty percent in the early 1980s. The number of Caribbean immigrants also increased during this period, from an average of 29,000 in the 1970s to 34,000 in the 1980s. During the period between the 1970s and early 1980s, Caribbean immigrants, in particular, accounted for one-third of the immigrant flow to Brooklyn (see Newest New Yorkers 1992). Some of central Brooklyn's neighborhoods (i.e., Flatbush, E. Flatbush, Crown Heights, Midwood, and Prospect Heights) had settlement concentrations between five and ten thousand Caribbean immigrants each. Specifically, in Brooklyn, Haitians were the largest entering group at the time. Jamaica and Guyana were the next largest. There was also a substantial presence of other Caribbean groups such as Trinidadians, Dominicans, Grenadians, Barbadians (Bajans), Panamanians, and Vincentians. Caribbean immigrants that settled in New York and in Brooklyn were much younger than the general immigrant population, with a median age of twenty-five. Traditionally, the search for economic opportunities fuels immigration, which is one reason why immigrants-- from poorer countries--tend to be younger than the general immigrant population. The sex ratio of these Caribbean immigrants averaged ninety males per one hundred females. More than half of these immigrants were married; one-third of whom had children under the age of five years. With regard to occupational characteristics, only twenty-five percent of Caribbean immigrants entering between 1972 and 1982 reported a professional specialty and technical occupation (e.g., engineers, doctors and nurses) or administrative support occupation (e.g., secretaries and bank tellers).

Female immigrants dominated service sector jobs as fabricators and laborers (e.g., sewing machine operators, tailors, and cooks), service workers (e.g., child care and household workers), and in administrative support (e.g., clerks and bookkeepers). Female Caribbean immigrants comprise twice the proportion of immigrants in these less skilled jobs. Groups with the highest representation in service occupations included Jamaicans, Panamanians, and Trinidadians with each around sixty percent.

In terms of educational attainment, a disproportionate number of Caribbean immigrants had educational levels equivalent to a high school diploma. Of the Caribbean immigrants who did not report occupational information on their visa applications were either unemployed (e.g., worked "under the table") or students. Jamaicans and Haitians, for example, had the highest proportion of students entering New York City with student visas.

Overall, immigrants from the Caribbean at this time were disproportionately young, female, married with small children, high school educated, and occupied service jobs. In many regards, these characteristics had an important effect on how well these immigrants were incorporated into society. These characteristics determined who could afford better health care, education, and overall, be more successful economically. Many of these immigrants settled in central Brooklyn, with the hope of making it in previously established Caribbean enclaves. Instead, many faced poor economic conditions and limited opportunities.

The Beginning

The inception of The Caribbean Service Center was spawned in part by the need of communities, particularly racial and ethnic, immigrant communities, to have access to social, economic, and health assistance for its members. Founder and former Executive Director of The Caribbean Service Center, Sharon Higgins, saw this need during her studies in Public Health Administration and Community Health at St. Joseph's College in Brooklyn New York, in the early 1970s. At the time, Sharon Higgins, a Jamaican immigrant nurse, and a group of other Caribbean immigrant women nurses in public health shared a commitment to improve accessibility to health-related and social services for New York's Caribbean immigrant, low income, and indigent people. These women were frustrated that the City's health care institutions and social organizations were failing to meet the needs of the immigrant population in Brooklyn. They found that this vastly growing Caribbean population residing in central Brooklyn neighborhoods also had poor access to medical services, an unhealthy living environment (i.e., increased exposure to environmental and occupational hazards), high levels of poverty and cultural and racial conflicts between whites and Blacks (see SUNY Downstate Medical Center Community Report: Archives 1992, 2000). In addition to these community characteristics, the nurses found that existing health and social services were unequipped with culturally relevant staff and services for Caribbean immigrants.

As nurses and health practitioners, Sharon Higgins and others found that hospitals and community health and social service centers lacked the necessary knowledge and skills to clearly explain how medical services were administered in the United States to a population of clients that were unfamiliar with American medical practices.

The hospitals' lack of cultural sensitivity pushed many immigrants and legal residents away from services. As a result, the hospitals saw high rates of Caribbean immigrant patients in the emergency room with ailments that would have been prevented had these patients sought

medical attention earlier.   The daily experiences of Caribbean people
not receiving adequate and appropriate services shaped the nurses'
grievances, established the measure of their demands, and pointed out
the targets of their anger. This situation prompted the nurses to meet
and brainstorm ways to address this concern on a broader level.

Concomitantly, the nurses were taking courses for a Master's in
Public Health Administration when they met with the then-doctoral
candidate and St. Joseph College's adjunct lecturer Dr. Gary Whits.
Together, the nurses and Dr. Gary Whits, also a Caribbean immigrant,
began to discuss plans for making changes in the health and social
services available to the central Brooklyn community.

On their own, they set up blood pressure drives using folding
chairs, tables, and signs, and placing them on the street corners of
shopping areas on Saturdays. Sharon Higgins believed that Saturday
drives were a way to access an untapped sector of the Caribbean
community by providing noninvasive services in a public setting,
without much question as to whether the passersby had health
insurance or not or were citizens or not. The idea was that the
passersby could stop, get free medical attention, and ask important
questions, while shopping with their families for food and clothes.

This effort was successful; many of the passersby seemed less
intimidated by the nurses because the latter were also Caribbean and
identified with and understood the culture and the perspective of
immigrants. Sharon Higgins explains,

> We knew that maneuvering the [health care] system and
> negotiating services can be very cumbersome and when the
> ability to pay is the main issue, then sometimes seeking help
> drives people away. And then these immigrants enter
> [hospitals] and are concerned about that [as well as] wow, you
> know, maybe this person--doctor or nurse--doesn't understand
> my definition of illness. But coming from a Caribbean
> background, we can relate to them. [Culturally], we identify
> pain on our body very differently. Our whole comfort zone
> with talking about our anatomy, various parts of our anatomy
> is problematic here in America. Knowing this, I have gone as
> far as writing down on paper the word 'vagina' and have some
> of the female patients say it aloud. And you can see they have
> issues and problems talking to their children, spouses, and

even doctors about those kinds of things-- because that's the way we, Caribbean people, are. We don't speak very openly about anything that has to do with our bodies, or sex or sexuality. So when [Caribbean] people come in to the [health care] system talking about their ailments, this is quite foreign to them. So, it was so important that as Caribbean nurses, we advocate, to help walk them through the system to get the help they needed.

The nurses continued to organize these drives on the weekends but soon realized that more needed to be done. They felt that as a small group, they were limited in the number of people they could help. The nurses began to feel overwhelmed by the positive response of the passersby to the extent that they received repeat clients, who came every week seeking medical advice and assistance. In collaboration with the nurses, Dr. Gary Whits helped to organize a conference on "Health and Caribbean Immigrants in New York City," which took place in 1981. Dr. Gary Whits and the nurses tapped into their social ties and networks within the Caribbean American community and rallied support from scholars, policy makers, health professionals and community leaders. These participants shared their interest in developing health care strategies that would be more responsive to the needs of the rapidly growing Caribbean population. From the perspective of Sharon Higgins, the conference was empowering.

I mean there were a lot of people there--academics, practitioners, other nurses and doctors who we [the nurses] worked with--all working together to help our people in the community. We weren't alone in noticing the persistent problems and we all felt the immediate need to act, to take control over the community, our community, when others didn't. During the conference, there was much talk and in the end there was a resolve--we needed to organize quickly for us, because who else will?

Participants shared a sense of togetherness which allowed them to brainstorm and frame some of the larger community issues as a collective. The sense of empowerment Sharon Higgins described opened the door to organizing for change. One of the outcomes of the conference was the recognition of the need for the creation of an organization whose main purpose was to advocate for, and provide health, immigrant, and social services for Caribbean and racial-ethnic migrant groups. The immediate concern for Dr. Gary Whits was that if the nurses' activities were to expand into an organization, their efforts should remain community oriented and as grassroots as possible. He felt that continuing to engage in grassroots, community oriented activity allowed the budding organization to maintain a strong connection to the community, and would lead to its ability to directly affect political and social change in the community. Dr. Gary Whits believed that organizing on the local level would provide the Caribbean community with resources and assistance from Caribbean practitioners and providers who share a common cultural affinity to assess their health and social experiences. In addition, he also recognized that maintaining a cultural connection to Caribbeans and the Caribbean experience would allow for the organization to rally support on bigger social issues such as racism, unemployment, and housing. Dr. Gary Whits adds,

...Organizing is a way of keeping in touch with the community and its pulse. When you are in the trenches, you see on the front line the suffering that takes place. Many of us in the community are undocumented and we, as organizers, see their plight every day. We're driven in terms of making a difference. We carry out campaigns and initiatives on a daily basis. It's not in the newspaper, it's not on the radio, but people bring their troubles when they come and lay that burden down. And that's what propels us in terms of advocating that way and of course, making a difference even on larger issues.

Dr. Gary Whits and Sharon Higgins's notion of collective identity-- Caribbean identity and culture-- was critical to the idea that Caribbean communities are worthy of political representation and support. The nurses believed that promoting Caribbean identity, and, in effect, Caribbean culture was a powerful strategy for reinforcing the impression that the Caribbean population was a viable community with a strong presence in Brooklyn and New York City. The nurses and their community supporters used their informal networks and relationships to provide the material resources needed for the nurses' mobilizing efforts to expand. To fully bring their efforts to the public, the nurses realized that the activities they engaged in--helping the sick and poor Caribbean immigrants in the area--needed public recognition. In effect, to receive public recognition increases the ability of current participants to recruit new individuals interested in supporting the movement agenda. The nurses and supporters opened their homes for meetings, used copiers from their day jobs to make fliers, involved their friends and families--children and spouses--in getting the word out to the public, and used their day employers to co-sponsor or provide resources for upcoming events.

For several months, the nurses and supporters worked together to frame their issues and goals and connect them to widely--held ideas the general public had about the changing demographics of New York City. Their first major task was to create a name for the developing organization. The name chosen symbolically represents both the politics of identity and the organizers' initial organizing purpose. The nurses, who founded and gave birth to the movement, wanted a name that represented their personal relationship with the community. Because the founders of the movement were Caribbean women who were concerned about healthcare and reducing health disparities for Caribbean people, they wanted an association whose long-term intent was to be a liaison to both the community and larger social institutions. Hence, the name of The Caribbean Service Center became a clear choice. Archibald Dubnet, Board member explains,

A name is critical; it is an identity-- how you're defined, how you're seen. You never want to misrepresent yourself or give the impression that you're something you're not. As a group, we were very clear as to who we're trying to serve and the changes we want to bring about in the community. It is about unity and not exclusion. For that, the challenge is always the name--as simple as it may seem. We finally decided on *The Caribbean Service Center* because it shows our commitment to the Caribbean community and that the services we want to provide will improve the entire community--Black American and immigrant alike.

During the movement's transition to a more bureaucratized entity, in non-confrontational terms, organizers focused on presenting their agenda of equitable health care and social services for racial-ethnic, Caribbean immigrant people to the general public. By publicly identifying with and sharing social concerns about the state of immigrant and citizen affairs, the movement had the opportunity to appeal to individuals and institutions outside of the Caribbean community that were also focused on the effects of international migration on the City. Based on public response, organizers knew their grassroots activity depended on the changing demographics in the City. The demographic changes created an opportunity structure for pan-ethnic groups and organizations to develop services to include the needs of the growing Caribbean population migrating to the city. According to resource mobilization theorists, changes within an opportunity structure enable social movements to expand and become more organized (see McCarthy and Zald 1973; Jenkins and Perrow 1977; Tilly 1979; Melucci 1985). As a result, the organizers took advantage of the opportunity structure and carved out a niche for the movement to develop into a formal organization, The Caribbean Service Center.

Role of the Media

To increase the size of their networks, organizers relied heavily on reaching and maintaining contact with leaders in and outside of the Caribbean community. These contacts would later prove to be critical for the new organization's funding. Organizers for the Caribbean Service Center saw media advocacy as an important strategy to frame persisting public health concerns, gain access to and mobilize the public and encourage policy makers to enact particular policy solutions, and at the same time, promote the organization and the services offered (see Abroms and Maibach 2008). Organizers also relied on media coverage to attract the attention of those willing to fund and support their new organization. In fact, organizers realized that using the media to catch public interest would increase their support from larger social service institutions, grantors, and appeal to public officials interested in expanding their constituency.

Dr. Gary Whits explains,

> From the beginning and even today, we need the media and because of this, we have to learn how to work it. We have to know who the big players are and how to target them and get their attention. Reporters and editors know who is who and who brings what. They know who brings results. It's now like a matter of credibility. We have to present ourselves, our agenda in such a way that will get us what we need--money, political support, community support--you know.

The Caribbean Service Center's media coverage appealed to the founders' own individual social network as well as targeted people most concerned with the increasing disparity in health care and social services for racial-ethnics and immigrants. Through radio and newspaper media, The Caribbean Service Center and its organizers developed a broader network and support from both African American and Caribbean leaders in the community and gained legitimacy within both the organizational environment and in the community. Media coverage also targeted potential clients, Blacks--both native and foreign born-- as a means to influence them and their social networks (i.e., good friends, spouses, and family members) to adopt recommended health behaviors and practices that would help to improve their access to and utilization of culturally competent care. In both instances, the media coverage The Caribbean Service Center received stimulated interpersonal communication between people within these social networks, encouraging them to discuss the development of this new organization. As a result, The Caribbean Service Center's organizers' ability to solicit support from African American leaders showed Caribbeans and others in the community that there were African Americans sympathetic to the challenges Caribbeans in the community faced.

Interestingly, the use of media also allowed African Americans in the central Brooklyn community to see that what they thought were primarily African American issues (e.g., discrimination, poverty, and unemployment) were not unique to them. Media coverage raised the consciousness of racial-ethnics in the community and encouraged the participation of other ethnics in The Caribbean Service Center's efforts to remediate problems that also affected Caribbeans. This attracted more Caribbeans to utilize the organization's services as well as lead to the expansion of its programs.

Using media coverage to promote the activity of the founders' movement and their developing Caribbean-based organization also caused complications. For example, social scientists (Glazer and Moynihan 1963) and journalists have used the media to suggest that Caribbean immigrants are adept businesspeople, hard working, and high achievers as a way to shape public opinions that Caribbean immigrants are more worthy of positive media representation than African Americans. Founders recognized that there were immediate gains and costs to improving Caribbean people's social status and their access to services by also improving their public image. According to Dubois (2003), Black ethnic communities, such as Caribbeans, have used the media to promote the more dignified aspects of their ethnic heritage (i.e., a hard work ethic). Using the media as a medium to pursue Caribbean status is more than posturing self-respect and pride but also requires Caribbeans to consider and promote its group's mastery of English, past citizenship and civic activity, personal initiatives, and suitable economic skills.

Yet, by explicitly promoting Caribbean heritage and improving its ethnic group status, a painful dilemma arises--the politics of "Blackness." In the face of racism towards African Americans in the United States, Caribbean community members have unconsciously and unintentionally internalized negative media representations that show American-born Blacks as lazy and being the pariahs of society. In effect, the media reinforced the perception that Caribbean people are better than African Americans by also subscribing to such racial stereotypes. Caribbeans sought to escape identification with African Americans so that they could be perceived as different, foreign, and therefore more acceptable than African Americans. Hence, media representations improved the status of Caribbean people by depicting them as being different from American-born Blacks and more worthy of particular news coverage.

Though unfortunate for African Americans, the founders' movement's explicit promotion of Caribbean heritage unintentionally benefited from positive media depictions of Caribbean people and the perpetuation of negative stereotypes against African Americans. Despite this negative media portrayal of African Americans, many African Americans and Caribbeans continued to support the founders' movement because they believed that the founders' goal was not to explicitly discriminate or exclude non-Caribbean populations. Instead, many of the movement's African American and Caribbean supporters believed that the media coverage received allowed the movement to achieve its public awareness goals of promoting the worthiness of Caribbeans and need for Caribbeans to receive health and social services, housing, employment, care for the sick and aged, safer streets, and a living wage. The movement gained legitimacy across the City. In less than a year, news articles and other publications, including *Carib News*, *The Daily News*, and *Ethnic Watch*, distributed across the City began to feature the community activities of the organizers. The media coverage the movement received put organizers in direct contact with grantors willing to fund the development of The Caribbean Service Center. By 1982, The Caribbean Service Center grew under Sharon Higgins's leadership. With twelve Caribbean nurses, Dr. Gary Whits, and other community leaders, and a budget of approximately $82,000, The Caribbean Service Center became a volunteer association, housed in one member's home. Many volunteered their time and efforts and worked without pay while balancing the responsibility of full-time jobs and family life. These early years were difficult but enabled organizers to focus on the social concerns (i.e., offering health clinics and counseling and referral services) that inspired them to organize in the first place.

The Movement's Transition to a Community-based Organization

Using tenets of Rothschild-Whitt's (1979:519-520) conception of collectivist organizing, I contend that the movement's transformation to The Caribbean Service Center was facilitated by like-minded individuals with minimal division of labor, rules, rewards or incentives. Collectivist organizing is when the interaction among the movement's organizers can be described as being a collective-- holistic, personalized, informal, with the intention to achieve group consensus. Solidarity also is necessary and especially a compelling incentive to people with strong moral commitments that can ethnically and racially understand the community it rallies for.

Scholars (Breines 1989; Rothschild-Whitt 1979) argue that collectivist organizing requires time consuming, decision making processes. Because the movement and its organizers were mostly women, who were married and had young children, collectivist activity could not be maintained. It was during this time that the transition of the grassroots movement to a more formal organization also began to include elements of bureaucratic organizing. The organizers sought the assistance of others focused on the same goals to assist their efforts. As more individuals became interested and involved in The Caribbean Service Center, organizational authority and hierarchy inevitably developed. One founder and current Board member, Dawn DeSousa explains,

It was really hard balancing family, my regular day job, and organizing. Organizing takes a lot of time and energy... I would say that Sharon Higgins's corporate model--getting incorporated, getting counsel, getting an accountant, getting government funding--made our efforts more effective and efficient. ...We, as a group, can do so much more. And so Sharon Higgins went with the corporate model side and did her lobbying...and it was just onward and forward. I guess I can speak for the rest of the founders when I say having a corporate model increased our effort potential overall. There was better communication amongst us and we were able to grow into the organization that we have today.

Within its first year, organizers focused their efforts on establishing clear, concrete organizational goals. By being more bureaucratic, the organizers established formal divisions of labor, rules and standards of performance, and hierarchal positions as a way to utilize all the efforts of those who participated. This type of organizing is designed for effectiveness--the ability to confront specific obstacles and seek concrete solutions (Aldrich 1999). Between 1981 and 1982, participants made personal loans ranging from three hundred dollars to tens of thousands of dollars to establish the organization. By the close of the first year, The Caribbean Service Center was serving almost 2,000 people in the community. This was considered a huge accomplishment by the organizers.

Another founding nurse and Board member, Vanessa Smith, explains,

> Dr. Gary Whits and I spoke last week regarding The Caribbean Service Center's upcoming events this summer and I thought to myself: Imagine that. We have made it so far from where we started. I remember being very nervous when borrowing money on my house, from my household savings, to come up with money to help start this organization. I look back and it was a wonderful thing. God was in the midst. To get enough money, in just a few months, to help so many people, was a miracle. I am sure of it.

With monies secured and an organizational niche being carved out for The Caribbean Service Center in the community, founders and organizers devised a mission statement and aim that still exists today:

- To provide comprehensive, culturally sensitive health care, immigration and support services to a diverse constituency; and,
- To improve the well being of individuals, to strengthen families and empower communities.

The establishment and promotion of this organizational mission and aim attracted both Caribbean immigrants and African Americans in the community. Caribbean immigrants were attracted to The Caribbean Service Center because of the organization's support for Caribbean people and their concerns. African Americans also were attracted to the organization because of its broad aim to support a diverse constituency. The initial attraction to the organization and subsequent participation by those in the community later helped to encourage the organization's broader political agenda of political, economic, and social empowerment. While the mission statement and organizational aim appeal to the broad ethnic composition of the central Brooklyn community, in reality, Caribbean people started The Caribbean Service Center and primarily focused on Caribbean immigrant issues in a large Caribbean immigrant and Caribbean American community. In effect, the founders' primary focus on Caribbean issues shaped The Caribbean Service Center's organizational ideology, staffing, culture and climate, and community relations.   Arguably, The Caribbean Service Center's primary focus on Caribbean immigrant issues may appear to be discriminatory towards non-Caribbean populations, however, founders assert The Caribbean Service Center's celebration of Caribbean pan-ethnicity is not intended to ostracize.

Instead, founders contend that African Americans and other racial-ethnic groups can look to The Caribbean Service Center as another venue to access and utilize services focused on uplifting the disenfranchised in community.

Founders devoted time and energy to developing an organizational structure and a programming agenda that would best serve to improve the well being of the Caribbean immigrant and racial-ethnic families in the community.   As with most bureaucracies, in order to maintain sustainability in the community and to be deeply committed to social change and better serving people, The Caribbean Service Center's took on an organizational structure with clear and centralized hierarchies of authority and responsibilities (see Aldrich 1999; Gerth and Mills 1958; Weber 1981).   Developing an organizational structure helped the organization's workers understand the chain of command and the flow of communication between themselves and other workers that were responsible for working with clients and managing the organization daily.   In effect, the structure clarified staff members' role in the organization.

The organizational structure is as follows (see Appendix A, Description of positions and Figure 6: Organizational Chart): Board of Directors, Community Leaders, an Executive Director, Administrative Assistant, Program Managers, Case Managers, and Volunteers/Outreach Assistants.   Specifically, the Board of Directors is responsible for leading and supervising the organization.   They do this through establishing the organizations aims, goals, and long-and short-term agendas.   Community leaders help articulate the needs and grievances of the community to the organization as well as assist the organization in remaining client-driven and community-focused.   The Executive Director has authority and discretion over hiring of staff, the everyday tasks and routines of the various programs and its managers, and conducting evaluations on quality and effectiveness of service. The Administrative Assistant performs clerical tasks, disseminates important information throughout the organization to staff members, and compiles press releases.   Program Managers set the short-term goals for their program and Case Managers carry out the service provision process. Finally, The Caribbean Service Center's Volunteers and Outreach Assistants assist program managers in everyday routines and tasks, and disseminate information regarding services directly to the community. With an organizational structure in place and The Caribbean Service Center's focus on Caribbean immigrant and Caribbean American issues, The Caribbean Service Center also helped to institutionalize a Caribbean ethnic presence in central Brooklyn. The collective identity of Caribbean life and culture in Brooklyn created a self-conscious, socially cohesive Caribbean community that promoted solidarity, self-help, and self-reliance. In doing so, The Caribbean Service Center was able to acquire clients and recruit more staff workers and volunteers that believed in the focus of the founders as well as the organization's mission. The founders targeted Caribbean immigrant women and their families as a way to solicit their support of The Caribbean Service Center and to legitimize the community organization as a Caribbean organization. Sharon Higgins was a frequent public speaker in central Brooklyn and an advocate of increasing services to Caribbeans--women and families. She also used her social and political platform to advocate for the collective political interests of the community's Caribbean members. Sharon Higgins noted,

Many of the Caribbean people coming to this country are women. Women are responsible for situating their families, their children, and providing a good home life. That's a huge burden. As a woman focused on these needs, as a Caribbean, as an immigrant woman sensitive to certain health and social issues that affect Black and immigrant women and their families, it is important that I am able to work with [staff workers, nurses, and community leaders] that are willing to do community health education, for example, urging these immigrant women to start early and continue prenatal care. Having a leadership position [in the community and in The Caribbean Service Center] is also important for new immigrants. They see me in a role that deals with corporate governance, marketing and political engagement. I serve as the link person to work with the congressional members, the legislative members, to help Caribbeans and women in the community.

As post-1965 immigrants, the founders' experiences were very similar to the population of clients The Caribbean Service Center initially targeted for services. Because the post-1965 migrant stream tends to be dominated by women like themselves--women focused on caring for husbands and children as well as maintaining ties to the Caribbean community both abroad and in the United States--the founders saw The Caribbean Service Center as a vehicle to support Caribbean immigrant women and Caribbean American people.

In general, a woman's departure for New York City and Brooklyn from the Caribbean requires more careful orchestration than a man's, and the support of kin, friends, and community is crucial for her and her family's survival. As wage earners, women are often the first members of a family to migrate and set up households. Hence, migrant women's network of kin, friends, and the community serve as invaluable sources of information for work, housing, child care and rearing, and protection and assistance to overcome the multiple obstacles of an unfamiliar city. A closer look at women's migrant experiences reveals that gender influences their social and economic mobility (for a broader discussion, see Anderson and Isaacs 2007; Jones 2008; Therborn 2004). In particular, Pessar (1999) and Watkins-Owens (2001) contend that Caribbean immigrant women relied more on their social and community networks when considering the well-being of their children and creating employment alternatives to low-wage and household work. These scholars suggest that, historically, Caribbean immigrant women have utilized their gender-based social networking skills brought with them from their home countries to establish child fostering networks, income earning enterprises, mutual aids societies, and rotating credit when they arrived to their host society. Therefore, without the assistance of community and social networks, Caribbean immigrant women would be vulnerable to poor living and economic conditions. In this regard, recognizing migrant women's need for strong community support made it possible for the founders of The Caribbean Service Center to reach out to Caribbean immigrant women and their families.

The First Decade

During its first decade of operations, The Caribbean Service Center expanded by instituting a myriad of programs and services. The first two services provided by the founders and their volunteers were health programs: maternal and child health and family health. Initially, these two health programs focused on case management and referral services. The delivery of these two services took place at the home of one of the founders. In addition to meeting clients at the founder's home, many of the founders who were nurses continued to travel to shopping areas and help clients on the street. After several months of extensive traveling to and from the shopping area and the home, the founders decided to search for a local site ideal for delivering services of all kinds. After a year of searching, the founders secured a location in the heart of central Brooklyn.

The First Decade: *Description of Site*

Set in the middle of an apartment-lined street block, The Caribbean Service Center planted its roots in one of Brooklyn's city-owned buildings. The building was off-white, Victorian style with large and wide steps in the front. A tall, iron black gate surrounded the building separating it from the red-brick seven-story apartment buildings adjacent on both sides. The Victorian style building was set back several feet from the sidewalk, creating a grand and stately appearance. On one side of the building was a parking lot; the front and side of the building were lined with grass, wooden benches and trees. The building had a total of four floors; each floor lined with large paneled windows. The building was large enough to accommodate sizeable office spaces for local politicians and leaders, and social service agencies. Founders selected one of the top floors of the building to rent for its office space. Prospective clients would enter The Caribbean Service Center's space and were welcomed by a large banner with the organization's name behind the front desk and waiting area. Located beneath the banner was the mantra "For the people by the people." The space had two large conference rooms, an activity room, designated client areas, a copy and administrative area, a small resource library, and several offices for staff members, including program managers, case workers, and volunteers/interns. In all, The Caribbean Service

Center occupied approximately six to eight thousand square feet of space.

Occupying one floor in this building put The Caribbean Service Center in touch with politicians and community leaders and gave the organization the opportunity to establish a rapport with individuals who are focused on the needs and concern of this diverse community. In addition, the building was located within five-minutes walking distance from three of Brooklyn's large hospitals. The Caribbean Service Center's close proximity to these three hospitals helped strengthen its ability to refer clients and receive support from major hospitals in the area.

The First Decade: *Description of Service Population*

According to confidential client records during The Caribbean Service Center's first decade, its service population comprised of a significant proportion of female, first generation Caribbean immigrants who recently migrated and lived in the United States for less than five years. Specifically, 78% of the organization's clients were female, and 22% male; the majority of clients was between the ages of seventeen and thirty-five and had some secondary school education. With regard to clients' socio-economic status, over 65% of clients were considered low income, with an average household income of $29.9K and less; 30% were considered working class, with household incomes between $30K and 45K; and 5% of the client population had incomes above $50K. The Caribbean Service Center's female clients had the highest labor force participation rates. Many were employed in the service sector or were domestic workers. Many of these women maintained households with children (both foreign-born and American) that were female headed.

The background characteristics of The Caribbean Service Center's clients mirror those of the general central Brooklyn community. Approximately 35% of the population legally qualified for and received food stamps, Medicaid, Supplemental Social Security (SSI), and other forms of public assistance. In that regard, many of the community's Caribbean immigrant clients needed services that targeted them--their children and families--and these immigrants sought health related social services made available to them at The Caribbean Service Center despite their resident status. In many ways, this initial expansion can be attributed to both the hard work of The Caribbean Service Center's staff workers and its founders' ability to solidify the organization's relationship with the Caribbean community as a Caribbean identified organization through advocacy and outreach. One can argue that the history of The Caribbean Service Center, which was based on the grassroots activity of a group of Caribbean nurses, set the stage for how the organization continues to connect with and represent the Caribbean community it serves.

The Caribbean Service Center's Social Movement History: Implications for Caribbean identity

When scholars (Cohen 1985; McAdams 1995; Tarrow 1994; Taylor and Whittier 1995) study social movements, they often focus on the emergence and maintenance of social movement organizations as well as their apex and eventual decline. Scholars such as Staggenborg (1998), on the other hand, argue that only focusing on the development of social movement organizations, as a unit of analysis, is insufficient. Instead, she suggests that including the social movement community (i.e., the individuals, and the formal and informal networks that comprise a community) allows scholars to conceive that social movements also consist of cultural groups as well as their economic and political activities. In many ways because of its grassroots history, The Caribbean Service Center is congruent with Staggenborg's notion of social movement communities.

Typical in its development, the social movement, which ultimately led to The Caribbean Service Center's inception, consisted of nurses, community leaders, educators, practitioners, and service providers held together by their social networks and ideologies. Because the development of The Caribbean Service Center also included informal networks of community activists--who shared and advanced the goals of the social movement without directly belonging to the organization-- it, in effect was a social movement community. A social movement community encompasses all actors who share and advance the movement regardless of whether or not they belong to the social movement organization. Social movement communities differ from social movement organizations in that they exist to provide services and educate the community in addition to politically advocating on its behalf. In effect, the notion of community for The Caribbean Service

Center here implies that mutual support exists among individuals
connected to Caribbeans in New York City and in central Brooklyn.
The key element connecting The Caribbean Service Center's social
movement community is culture. The element of culture and
particularly Caribbean culture--in the sense of symbols, rituals, and
ideology--is shared and developed by individuals within the
community, the movement, and within The Caribbean Service Center
itself, which lends itself to the formation of a collective Caribbean
identity.

The idea of a common "we-ness," a set of shared beliefs,
understandings, and interests constructed in interaction between and
among The Caribbean Service Center's nurses, founders, and other
movement participants, has helped to introduce Caribbean culture as a
variable of collective action. The concept of a Caribbean collective
identity is useful in understanding the nature of connection that still
exists between Caribbeans involved in the nurses' grassroots movement
and those that continue to support The Caribbean Service Center.
Social movement theorists Melucci (1996) and Cohen (1985) suggest
that culture-building and identity are an integral part to collective
identity formation in any type of social movement. Collective identity
is defined as the socially constructed "shared definition of a group that
derives from members' common interests, experiences and solidarity
constructed through interaction in the community" (Taylor and Whittier
1995:172). According to Valocchi (2001:448), "implicit in this
constructionist definition of collective identity is a definition of
ideology shaped by the individuals themselves as they become aware of
commonalities, establish interpretive frameworks that emphasize these
commonalities, and build communities or social networks to reinforce
these commonalities" (see also Rupp and Taylor 1999).

As part of activity building, the nurses' concept of a Caribbean
collective identity included common language, a common territory, and
a common psychology and culture of the Caribbean basin. They use
this concept of identity to organize Caribbeans along both ethnic and
class lines (i.e., working class, middle class, and upper class). For the
nurses, bringing Caribbean medical and social needs and concerns to
the forefront of the dialogue on the social, health, economic, and
political subordination of Blacks in central Brooklyn and the broader
New York City community was, as they saw it, necessary to

fundamentally changing the distribution of resources and services allocated to diverse Caribbean immigrant and ethnic communities.

As The Caribbean Service Center became institutionalized over time, collective ideology and collective identity remained a critical factor in mobilizing the Caribbean community. With the internalized set of meanings attached to Caribbean collective identity, the founders ensured that these meanings are oriented to validate The Caribbean Service Center in the community. Snow and McAdams (2001: 49-53) suggest that when such an identity is institutionalized into an organization's structure, collective identity must remain fluid, so that individuals can continue to come together around common grievances, interests, or social ties, and engage in dialogue and activity. While Caribbean ethnicity is diverse—rooted in African, British, French, and Hispanic ancestry, language, and culture-- the nurses' and other organizers' ability to recruit Caribbeans continues to be successful because the founders appeal to these diverse Caribbeans' multiethnic identities. Founders refashion these identities by incorporating various cultural elements of each identity into a more broad-based Caribbean ethnic identity.

The conception of collective Caribbean identity that enabled the collective action of the nurses, founders, and the recruitment of participants, in many ways, is an integral element to The Caribbean Service Center's grassroots maintenance and continuity. In fact, the social movement, which led to the development of The Caribbean Service Center built upon the nurses' and founders' commitment and connection to the Caribbean community and solidified the organization's role in and commitment to the central Brooklyn Caribbean immigrant community that exists today. The Caribbean Service Center's founders and staff continue their activism in the Caribbean community through the organization by establishing and promoting Caribbean ideology and culture as well as providing programming and services that are rooted in grassroots action. In this regard, The Caribbean Service Center became more than a locale to access and receive free or low-cost services; instead The Caribbean Service Center became a gathering place for Caribbeans to unite and mobilize.

For Caribbean and racial-ethnic, immigrant clients and community members, the nurses' and founders' personal commitments to the Caribbean community are easily identifiable. The Caribbean Service

Center was founded by Caribbeans, is centered on serving Caribbeans and creates visibility for a Caribbean social movement. The community's perception of the nurses' and founders' personal commitment to the community makes it easier to attract more participants, supporters, and clients to The Caribbean Service Center. Since The Caribbean Service Center's inception as a grassroots movement to a community-based organization, its organizers had to interpret the world around them, frame their ideas, and emphasize efforts that connect to the self-conceptions, values, or moral and cultural sensibilities of the community they hoped to serve (Trickett 2009). In order to effectively connect to the community, its organizers had to be able to identify with the experiences of the community as a means to mobilize and appeal to its members. In many regards, the broader ideologies that defined the orientations and aims of this movement were rooted in emotion. It was and continues to be the emotional connection to Caribbean people, albeit the issues and struggles faced by racial-ethnic immigrants, which is the important mechanism that stimulated and sustained founders' grassroots efforts and subsequent The Caribbean Service Center's development. In other words, the grievance of the Caribbean nurses, their collective Caribbean identity, and opportunity to organize was a perfect context to mobilize and formally organize around issues that relate to health and racial disparities for Caribbean immigrants in Brooklyn. Because their collective action was in large part based on ethnic identity, those that chose to work for and with The Caribbean Service Center inevitably attracted others (workers and clients) that also support Caribbean issues and desire improved delivery of social services to the broader community.

Legacies of Race and Immigrant-based Policies and the Expansion of The Caribbean Service Center

The Caribbean Service Center's social movement history laid the groundwork for the development and expansion of its programs and services during its early years. Founders sustained The Caribbean Service Center's grassroots elements through balancing service provisions with ethnic advocacy. This combination also helped to establish The Caribbean Service Center's organizational culture and climate, ideology, organizational activities, and staff approaches-- which are all critical elements of organization service provision. For the founders, expanding The Caribbean Service Center's programming activities was a complex feat that was often constrained by the organization's political, social, and economic environment.

According to Lipsky (1980), the determinants of street level practice--as conducted by community-based organizations--are deeply rooted in the structure of its environment (see also DiMaggio and Anheier 1990). Lipsky (1980:192) argued, "street level bureaucracies do not stand alone, but reflect the character of prevailing organizational relations in society as a whole." He suggested that community-based organizations are the primary instrument of contact between the government and the people, and these organizations reinforce the relationship between the community and both clients and workers and local politics. Hence, an organization's ability to provide the community with resources depends on its capacity to navigate through

national and local policy.   National and local policies can limit or
enhance an organization's programming and functioning, access to
federal and state funds, and its ability to effectively handle client case
loads.   During The Caribbean Service Center's first two decades of
operation, the founders' actions to expand the organization's activities
and programming to target central Brooklyn's Caribbean immigrants
and other populations of color--the working poor, undocumented illegal
aliens, and those who needed medical assistance but could not afford it-
-were impacted by post-1965 federal and New York state immigration
policy mandates.   These mandates influenced the types of programming
and service provisions The Caribbean Service Center was able to offer
their immigrant client population.

Central to understanding how The Caribbean Service Center
established an organizational context--a culture, climate, and an
ideology--that support the ethnic identity options and assertions of its
Caribbean immigrant clients is to also examine the ways post-1965
immigration policies shaped the socio-political context of its service
delivery system.   On the one hand, the founders' attempt to formalize
their grassroots efforts into a community-based organization is based,
in large part, on the salient experiences of race, ethnicity, and
immigrant status which gave rise to the desire to create The Caribbean
Service Center.   On the other hand, the founders' own identification
with a set of experiences they shared with other Caribbean immigrants
does not fully explain their ability to expand its efforts and maintain an
organization for three decades.

In the course of my research, it became clear that focusing on the
ways The Caribbean Service Center navigated through federal and
state-level immigration policy mandates while attempting to provide
culturally relevant services to Caribbean immigrants also meant
identifying its initial program initiatives and the types of services that
developed reinforced the organization's Caribbean identity and
ideology.   In this chapter, I argue that the 1965 amendment to the
Immigration and Nationality Act, which resulted in increased
heterogeneity of today's foreign-born residents by national origin as
well as ethnic and racial composition, informed The Caribbean Service
Center's Caribbean founders' understanding of the cultural and racial
ideologies that exist within New York City's human service sector.   I
suggest that the founders' understanding of these policies--both as
social service providers and as residents of the local Caribbean

community--impacted their decisions to offer programming that they believe best benefited their Caribbean immigrant clients.

Federal Immigration Policy

The federal government seeks to ensure that immigration policies serve the economic and social needs of the country. Federal immigrant policies have five goals: to enforce immigration policies; secure individual rights and grant equal protection; mitigate social services costs; reimburse state and local governments; and assist in the settlement and integration of the newly arrived. In effect, the federal government reserves the right to use subjective criteria to decide which immigrant groups they believe will and will not create "social problems" and economic burdens for the United States and its citizens (Briggs 1984).

Since the late 1870s, the federal government has used subjective criteria to determine which immigrants are allowed to enter the United States. For example, between the late 1870s through 1910, the federal government added admission qualifications to immigration laws as a way to deal with Irish, Mexican, Chinese, and Japanese immigrants entering the country. Because the rise in immigration of these immigrant groups overlapped with a time of economic problems and high levels of unemployment, the government saw them as "obnoxious immigrants"--persons who were destitute, active in immoral activities or physically handicapped--and limited them from entering the country (see United States Immigrants and Naturalization Service 1991a).

In 1921 and 1924, the federal government added admission qualifications that also restricted immigrant groups by their race, ethnicity, and national origin. These policies were one of the first federal mandates that determined immigrant worthiness by these categories. In 1952, the Immigration and Nationality Act, also known as the McCarran-Walter Act of 1952, removed these blatant racial restrictions for admission but retained the national origin restrictions of the 1921 and 1924 Acts. In addition, this act restricted the immigration of people from non-sovereign countries to America. While this act removed race and ethnic background as a criterion for admission, many of the non-sovereign countries the federal government prohibited admission from included non-white majority countries located in

Africa, Asia, and the Caribbean. Thus, federal government maintained control over the number of racial-ethnic groups entering the country. Immigration reforms occurred in 1963 when President John F. Kennedy proposed a revision and update of national immigration policies. The reforms, which became amendments to the McCarran-Walter Act, became the Immigration Act of 1965. The 1965 reform abandoned national origin restrictions and gave special provisions specifically for relatives of United States citizens and legal residents of Southern and Eastern European descent under the Family Reunification Act. By adding parents to the category of "immediate family members," and adding provisional categories for immigrants declaring specific statuses (related to war, work, education, and family), the idea was that the 1965 reform would enhance increased numbers of European immigrants into the United States (Keely 1990; United States Immigrants and Naturalization Service).

Policy makers' idea of increasing diversity among immigrants was intended to address the issue of the decreasing domestic white population as the racial-ethnic minority, foreign born population increased (Edmonston and Passel 1994). By changing the criteria with which European immigrants were admitted, the reform actually generated massive refugee flows into the United States and contributed to the non-white mix of the foreign-born population residing in the country (Keely 1990; Handlin 1973). In other words, the reform's emphasis on family reunification as an alternative to the national origin restriction, as the basis of admission, paved the way for Asian, South American, Caribbean and African immigration to increase dramatically in the United States over the last three decades. In fact, between 1965 and 1994, legal immigration from Asia, Latin America, and the Caribbean constituted over 80% of all legal immigration to the United States (The Newest New Yorkers: NYC Dept. of Planning 1996).

Notwithstanding policy makers' intention of increasing European immigration, the rate of these "new immigrants" entering the United States called for policy analysts to focus on the assimilation and acculturation process of the new racial-ethnic, immigrants and the communities they joined. State and local policy makers, in particular, were faced with the implications of federal immigration.

State and Local Immigration Policy

The federal government, however, is not alone in shaping immigration policy (Kraly 1987). State and local governments play a variety of roles that shape policy, including: implementing federal policy, setting benefit levels for joint federal-state programs, running independent programs and institutions targeted to newcomers, and setting benefit and eligibility standards for state and local programs and services to fit the needs of newcomers. There are two main factors or assumptions that influence how state and local governments implement federal policies. These factors or assumptions are primarily based on: (1) the social importance of race and ethnicity; and (2) race and ethnic-based international and domestic policies and its effect on fiscal expenditures. According to Glazer and Moynihan (1975:23) "immigration [policy] regulates the ethnic composition of the American electorate as well as responds to that ethnic composition. It responds to other things, but probably first of all to the primal factor of ethnicity." Federal immigration policy evaluates who is worthy of receiving social services.

To illustrate the different values placed upon similar racial-ethnic immigrant populations that resulted in various ways state and local governments addressed and met the needs of these immigrant groups, I will cite the U.S. government's treatment of Haitians and Cubans. For Cubans, the incentives for the United States to intervene on behalf of Cuban refugees would: (1) reaffirm the moral worth and virtuous image of America that "helped" refugees from communism; and (2) allow a large concentration of Cubans into the United States that would work to help overthrow the Cuban government. Since the Reagan Administration, the United States government was determined to stop the flow of Haitians into the country as a way to combat the increased numbers of minority immigrants in its borders. At the time, Haitians were the largest Caribbean immigrant population entering the United States. Many Haitians arriving required more resources than the United States government was willing to give. To reduce the number of Haitian immigrants, the Reagan Administration Reagan went so far as to get the Jean Claude Duvalier regime to prohibit U.S.-Haitian migration in exchange for general economic support.

What is apparent in these two examples is that the United States made particular choices with regard to foreign policy and strategy: Cubans, who were more affluent immigrants in comparison to Haitian immigrants, were seen as less of a social and economic burden (see Dominquez 1991; Sechzer and Ngang 1991). As a population at the lower end of the economic totem, Black immigrants from Haiti were deemed less worthy to receive services.

Haitian immigrants were not the only immigrants at the time that were deemed to be social and economic burdens to the United States. In fact, with a given rate of approximately one million documented immigrants and countless undocumented "brown" and "black," working class immigrants hailing from Mexico, Asia, Latin America and the Caribbean annually, Congress passed the Immigration Reform and Control Act of 1986 in response to the increasing number of these immigrants. By 1990, former President George H. Bush signed a new amendment to the 1965 Immigration and Nationality Act into law, which did not take full effect until 1995. The Immigration Act of 1990 established a visa allocation system that was based on America's need to have a greater "diversity in the nationality mix." The premise in allowing for more diverse, professional immigrants to enter the country was to offset immigrant-related costs for federal and state governments. The visa allocation system established flexible annual immigration levels of approximately 700,000 immigrants between years 1992-1994 and approximately 675,000 immigrants after 1995. While many Caribbean immigrants, for example, who emigrated from the islands, were either of working or middle class backgrounds, they had varying degrees of work and educational attainment levels, and were able to enter the country under this Act (see Bryce-Laporte 1985).

Congress, in its efforts to combat an immigrant surge of poor or working class brown and black people entering its borders, passed The Immigration Act of 1996. The 1996 act reinforced the severity of the 1986 act by allowing for the expedited removal of immigrants. Under the 1996 provision: (1) if legal permanent residents neglect to fill out paper work or commit petty crimes, they are liable to be treated like common criminals and deported abruptly; (2) residency requirements increased from 7 years to 10 years, eliminated hardship to the refugee as a basis to fight deportation, and limited the number of immigrants who could seek permanent residency; (3) imposed a 10 year bar of reentry on those who leave the country and forced them to return to

their home countries to obtain permanent visas; (4) required those
seeking to bring relatives here to meet income requirements and to
make legally enforceable promises to support newcomers. In 1997,
Congress and former President Clinton attempted to improve
America's, once again, tainted international image and decided to curb
aspects of the law, although many components still remained.

In working with the federal government, state and local
governments also choose to make investments in the human capital
(e.g., education and employment training) and social and health needs
of immigrants who are allowed to enter the United States. From the
1970s through the 1990s, New York experienced significant
demographic shifts of foreign-born populations as a result of American
Immigration Acts passed in 1965, 1986, 1990, and 1996. According to
Youssef (1992), immigrant statistics show that countries from the
Anglophone Caribbean (e.g., Jamaica, Trinidad and Tobago, Guyana,
Barbados, St. Vincent, and Grenada) supplied a significant number of
New York City's foreign born. He suggests that the significant increase
of immigrants from these countries to the United States, and
particularly to New York, was due to Great Britain's refusal to further
accept immigrants from former Black Commonwealth nations who
fought and won their independence.

New York State and City policy makers examined census data,
which recorded entrance rates of residents, illegal and legal immigrants,
and various kinds of refugees and deportees, to assess the types of
programs and the amount of funds organizations require to aid these
recent immigrants. The strategic determination of state and city-level
programming for immigrants is based on the definitions of racial
classifications of immigrants in the census. Since 1965, there have
been some changes in the way the U.S. census define, identify, and
group immigrants. For example, the 1970 census listed six regions of
origin (three of which are European) and a large listing of individual
European countries of origin. The classification by race included only
white, Black, and other. The 1980 census, however, listed five regions
of birthplace, twenty-six countries and over thirteen classifications by
race and ethnicity. The 1990 census also attempted to meet increased
data needs by including a "West Indian" category and related sub-
category ancestry group (i.e., Jamaican). It must be noted that issues of
census undercount is a persisting concern for those that fall into the
West Indian ancestry category because of its difficulty and cost.

Undercount is estimated by doing a post-enumeration of sample surveys of populations believed to be undercounted due to insufficient access. In 1991, the Secretary of the Department of Commerce decided not to adjust the 1990 census for undercount errors despite a recommendation for such an adjustment by the Director of the Bureau of the Census.

In addition to the growing diversity of new immigrants entering the country, analysts recognized that the condition of the American economy also creates vast changes in the kind of social welfare states can provide to new arrivals. In the national recession of the 1980s, New York State, for instance, lost federal funds for immigrant programming and had to replace these funds with state funds. In order to redistribute diminished monies, New York's Governor and state legislators cut benefits for low-income, racial-ethnic immigrants more drastically than they had ever done (Pickus 1998). In fact, these cuts reduced the number of programs designed specifically to serve racial-ethnic immigrants' needs as well as reduced the number of social organizations that existed at the state and local level that advocate for new immigrants (Howe 1990). As a result, New York's state and local governments were restricted by the federal government regarding cash and medical benefits, employment, housing, and accessibility to social services.

New immigrants internalized these restrictions to mean that the federal government did not value their plight and, as a result, believed there was less of an incentive for the federal government to do all that it could to assist them. The extent to which the federal government was willing to assist new immigrants was evident in the degree to which immigrants were made eligible for mainstream social assistance on the state and local levels. New immigrants must satisfy certain eligibility requirements in order to receive social service benefits. According to Wheeler (1988), various racial and ethnic immigrants groups have been effectively discouraged from accessing and utilizing federally funded, state mandated programs such as welfare. Many are told or are made to believe that reliance on government programs will make it more difficult to bring family members to the country. Often these immigrants do not disclose or are not forthcoming about their immigrant status when attempting to receive benefits. The lack of use of immigrant-sponsored state programs resulted in many programs' increased budget cuts.

With the reduced number of programs and services available to racial-ethnic immigrants, such as Caribbean immigrants, many of these people struggled to overcome health, social, and economic hardships because of limited resources and lack of social services. Thus, many Caribbean immigrants sought out members of the community for individuals and organizations, like The Caribbean Service Center, that understood their need for services for better living in order to receive the assistance they needed.

When it comes to understanding American immigration policy, one fact remains clear: the federal government can limit the power of state and local agencies in their efforts to assist new immigrants. This relationship between the federal government and state and local agencies is a key component to understanding how social organizations are limited in their ability to meet the needs and concerns of immigrants. In other words, an organization's ability to meet the needs of their clients is dependent upon the state's economy, racial-ethnic dynamics and composition, and access to federal funding. New York's state and city policies became extremely important to The Caribbean Service Center that serves a large racial-ethnic immigrant population.

New York Immigration Policy's effect on The Caribbean Service Center's Expansion

Federal and state-level budgets affected the quality of culturally relevant services and equity of opportunity for the central Brooklyn Caribbean community. As residents and social providers, The Caribbean Service Center's founders knew that the Caribbean community does not amass as many culturally competent resources as it needs. They knew that the Caribbean community would end up competing with other similarly impoverished and marginalized immigrant communities for resources, so they had to act quickly. To do this, the founders filed paperwork for The Caribbean Service Center to become accredited as a nonprofit organization. Juan Carlos, a Board member explains,

> At its start-up, CSC [Caribbean Service Center] had to move quickly. New nonprofits do not have the luxury of moving slowly when seeking funding opportunities. Grants do not stay around for long and competition can be pretty thick at times.

All organizations that serve communities in need are looking to apply for the same funds as us. Some of these organizations have been around longer and know the game better. Like anything, this was a necessary step to moving along CSC's efforts.

Filing as a nonprofit organization helped The Caribbean Service Center gain access to more funding opportunities and assistance from public and private agencies. At the time of its incorporation, federal and state-level grant opportunities available to community-based organizations like The Caribbean Service Center focused on maternal and child health. There were other grant opportunities available that focused on improving women's health through outreach and immigration services. Taking into account the community's need for services and the funding opportunities available, The Caribbean Service Center developed its first two health programs--maternal and child health, and family health.

Programs such as maternal and child health and family health provide case management and referral services, client education and counseling, and assist in the acquisition of improved services in mainstream hospitals. The organization's health programs were designed by using the founders' experiences as nurses and their knowledge of human services in central Brooklyn for Caribbean immigrants. Over the next two decades, The Caribbean Service Center would expand on these health programs to focus on perinatal care and parent education, a healthy start for children, managed care and home visits for children (see Appendix D: Detailed Description of Programming and Services).

The founders immediately saw the impact that changes in federal and state immigration policies had on the lives of their clients. With federal and state policies defining who is eligible for benefits, many of The Caribbean Service Center's community members and immigrant clients could not access the health and social services they needed most. Some clients and their family members had visas that were expired and as a result, faced deportation while others were denied services because of their green card status. Because many of the clients' immigrant status often served as a barrier to their access to services, founders saw the importance of assisting clients resolve their immigration issues to increase client access to support services. The Caribbean Service Center also became qualified as an Immigration and

Naturalization Service Designated Entity, allowing the organization to serve as a "safe haven" for immigrants seeking amnesty and social service assistance. This status allowed The Caribbean Service Center to potentially reach out to thousands of immigrants and assist them in resolving any immigration problems that prohibited them from accessing and utilizing health and social services.

As its third program, The Caribbean Service Center developed and continues to operate a nonprofit Immigrant Service program. The Immigration program is accredited to represent clients before the U.S. Immigration and Naturalization Services, the Immigration Court, and the Board of Immigration Appeals. The program helps to protect immigrant rights, assist immigrant clients in making positive adjustments and becoming self-sufficient productive members in their host communities while also offering low-cost legal services regardless of the immigrant's status or ethnicity throughout central Brooklyn and the larger New York City community.

The Caribbean Service Center's fourth program, Community Outreach, is the mainstay of the organization. The organization's ability to connect to the Caribbean community continues to be at the heart of The Caribbean Service Center's goal of ethnic advocacy. The Caribbean Service Center's ability to expand services over two decades was based on this connection to the Caribbean community. Patricia Habeem, a Program Manager explains,

> The growth of The Caribbean Service Center evolved because we are in fact, a community-based ethnic organization and [are] influenced by what happens at the community level. So for example, when The Caribbean Service Center started its prenatal outreach program, we knew that one of the biggest problems for Black, immigrant women was their access to prenatal care, due to their immigration status, and we had to combat that somehow. Then the federal government passed the 1986 Immigration Reform and Control Act. Included in the act were certain provisions that allowed CBOs [community-based organizations] to become qualified designated entities and offer immigration services; for us at The Caribbean Service Center, this was just the carrot for us. So we combined health and immigration. We were serving immigrants and more of them needed immigration services

before they can gain access to health services. So, we were able to triage them and connect them. And then, right after that, the AIDS epidemic became the new public health issue and many of our clients from the maternal child health programs and community residents started to come in to know what AIDS/ SIDA is. So then we realized that now we had to respond to these issues. And so it [The Caribbean Service Center] grew.

According to Dr. Gary Whits, "in order to be effective ethnic advocates, asserting a cultural identity is a necessary strategy to organize and be able to provide actual services." Helping their Caribbean clients maintain a connection to their home societies while building a new connection to American society has been an integral part of The Caribbean Service Center's efforts in being an agency for Caribbean people. Dr. Gary Whits claims that "we know many of us go back and forth to the Caribbean, so as an organization, we have to understand the realities of this transmigration and adapt." Hence, in addition to developing health and immigrant programming, The Caribbean Service Center expanded its programming activities to promote strong connections to Caribbean communities, both in the United States and abroad.

By the early 1990s, The Caribbean Service Center became accredited as a nongovernmental organization (NGO) by the United Nations Economic and Social Council (ECOSOC). The Caribbean Service Center continues to work with the United Nations and other community activists, academicians, clinicians, and policy makers in the Caribbean region and Latin America that are focused on supporting political and economic empowerment of Caribbean people around the world.

Having this connection to the Caribbean basin means a lot to The Caribbean Service Center's staff, founders, and current Executive Director. Its founders and current staff members believe that the organization's strong Caribbean connection to the people they serve has led to its long-term and continued success since its inception.

Charleene MacDonald, co-founder and current Board member explains,

> Over the decades we [The Caribbean Service Center] have been successful because we have maintained certain values and principles from day one. For example, we have defined what we mean by Caribbean, which is not just the island location but also what it means to be Caribbean here, in the mainland. We also check with the folks of the community, here and abroad. We maintain a cross-national board of directors who are a governing force in the organization and will make sure someone from Trinidad will have a formula, just like someone from here or someone from there will also have a formula or a voice, so we don't have a predominance of the organization's ideals or values representing one group of people, we have all.

In particular, Alex Acevedo, a community leader and activist, and LaShawna Minks, a case manager for the Asthma Program, have observed that The Caribbean Service Center is considered, among clients and many community members, an organization that openly supports and strongly identifies with the Caribbean community. LaShawna Minks goes on to add,

> I think that we know first hand as immigrants that immigrants have specific needs...or certain barriers so we do try to tailor it...So that's like a cultural thing. We have an understanding of these feelings and ideas and can best help our clients. We try to find the appropriate support for them. We know they are confident in us because they show up and want me and my staff to help.

Board member Marshall Jones suggests that The Caribbean Service Center's success is also based on its ability to be an organization for the community. He adds,

> For The Caribbean Service Center to be a community enterprise, it has to have roots in the community, not just an organization the community will find useful. The organization

would have to share the community's visions, interests, aspirations, and goals. That's what makes The Caribbean Service Center a community-based organization rather than an organization based in the community. There are institutions based in our community--like, for example, schools. If we [The Caribbean Service Center] work for parent empowerment, for parents to gain some control of the school, to gain some control of the curriculum, to gain some relationship with the school system, and are able to make demands for better resources for the children, then, in fact, the school is a community school. Otherwise it's just a school located in the community and nothing else. At The Caribbean Service Center, we are part of the heart of Brooklyn's Caribbean community as well as part of the community too.

Utilizing the insights of long-time community leaders and outreach workers in the Caribbean immigrant community of central Brooklyn, such as Alex Acevedo, Christopher Jones, Francois Toussaint, Erica Parke, and Rita David, enabled the Organization to retain many of the founders' initial social movement goals and aims--centrally focused on better serving Caribbean immigrants and their families. Throughout the 1990s, The Caribbean Service Center forged strong partnerships with religious organizations, schools, community boards and police; all viable social institutions in the Caribbean community both in central Brooklyn and City-wide. The Caribbean Service Center used these partnerships as a way to co-sponsor community initiatives and activities that the organizations could not handle on their own. Through these activities, The Caribbean Service Center continued to gain a sense of the needs of the community and expand its programming.

In the last ten years, The Caribbean Service Center expanded in size and programming. Today, The Caribbean Service Center has over 50 paid staff members, five service centers in central Brooklyn and Queens serving over 40,000 clients annually, and an average annual budget of $4 million. The organization's client population is approximately 85% Caribbean immigrant and Caribbean American, 10% African American, and 2-5% Asian and European immigrant. The Caribbean Service Center's clients today share similar socio-demographic characteristics of Caribbean immigrants the organization served during its first ten years. The majority of The Caribbean

Service Center's clients are women who are heads of households, recent immigrants (within the last 5-7 years), and considered low income despite their high labor force participation rates. As it was in the beginning, The Caribbean Service Center's expansion of programming and services reflected the needs and concerns of their immigrant constituency. Currently, The Caribbean Service Center has a total of seven main programs: maternal and child health, HIV/AIDS education and case management, environmental health, adolescent health, domestic violence, immigration, and primary care. In addition, The Caribbean Service Center also maintains several ancillary programs that focus on, for example, advocacy, outreach, and youth services. In 2000, The Caribbean Service Center was deemed by the Press Association for Nonprofits as "a leading nonprofit, immigration and social service advocacy agency that is recognized on the local, national, and international level as a pioneer in providing culturally sensitive services to diverse groups."

The Caribbean Service Center's continued sustainability in central Brooklyn's Caribbean community can be attributed to its ability to maintain its connection to the Caribbean community by emphasizing its belief that Caribbean people, and their needs and culture, are important. Like other ethnic-based community-based organizations, however, The Caribbean Service Center faced many obstacles in the external funding environment. These obstacles can be attributed to New York State policy mandates. The solutions that The Caribbean Service Center devised to combat these obstacles were based on the organization's ability to develop partnerships with external agencies to acquire resources, and its ability to relate to its service population.

The Caribbean Service Center's Interpretation of New York Immigration Policy: Obstacles & Solutions

As with any grassroots organization, the ability to provide services and advocacy is dependent upon financial resources. The Caribbean Service Center took advantage of existing funding opportunities within the local New York City government and applied for various grants that support organizational efforts geared toward improving the well-being of racial-ethnics, immigrants, and the working poor. For example, during the late 1980s and early 1990s, the borough of Brooklyn and the State of New York experienced a rising incidence of high infant mortality and HIV and AIDS diagnoses amongst Caribbean, including Hispanic/Latino, and Black American populations. As part of New York's own initiatives to combat these social concerns, The Caribbean Service Center received public funds through the NYS Department of Health: Perinatal Health Unit, AIDS Institute, AIDS Minority Initiative, HIV Counseling Program, Division of Nutrition; and the United States Department of Health and Human Services: Federal Centers for Disease Control and Prevention. With these resources, The Caribbean Service Center took advantage of fiscal opportunities and expanded programs that were necessary for assisting the community.

While there were funding opportunities to expand service provision, there were other areas where fiscal pressures forced The Caribbean Service Center to become more strategic in its operations. $3.5 million of The Caribbean Service Center's operating budget of $4 million per year comes from public sources. Public funds can be at times unreliable. With New York State immigration policy changes and budget cuts, The Caribbean Service Center's programs experienced shifts in their fund allotments.

According to The Caribbean Service Center's financial records, for fiscal years 1995 through 1999 grant allocation for the Immigrant Program increased from 5% to almost 12% with revenues and support (i.e., government, corporate and individual contributions and special events) totaling between $2 and $3 million per year. Between 2000 and 2002, grant allocation for the Immigrant Program decreased from 12% to 2% and then leveled off to 5% of total revenues and support used for program development and services. In contrast to these changes, the percentage of monies allocated to the Maternal Child Health Program and the HIV/AIDS Education and Prevention Program increased, ranging between 34 and 48% respectively between 1995 and 2002. The Board and Dr. Gary Whits knew that these shifts in fiscal allocations for The Caribbean Service Center's immigration program could be linked to federal and state immigration policies, which reflect the shift in the government's priorities for immigrant well-being to maternal health and HIV/AIDS awareness. Recognizing that The Caribbean Service Center's funding will always rely heavily on the financial support of the federal, New York State, and local governments, the Board and Dr. Gary Whits devised two major solutions to combat resource inadequacy that were also in compliance with The Caribbean Service Center's goals.

First, with the assistance of community leaders, the Board assessed and created additional ancillary programs (see Appendix C: Detailed Description of Programming and Services) to show there was a community demand for particular, culturally relevant services. Once the demand was present, the Board devised programming guidelines to meet funding criteria for new federal and state government grants. Using the recently acquired funds, new services were made available and current clients were channeled into these new programs. By moving clients to these new programs, The Caribbean Service Center used the new funds, in part, to handle previous programs' activities while adhering to grant guidelines. In other words, developing new programs and receiving funds for them is, in part, a guise to assist programs that have fewer monies allocated to them. Lenroy Reynolds, a Board member explains,

> In the community, leaders place fliers up notifying residents of changes in legislation and how such changes affect them. When immigration policies change, it affects the Caribbean men, women, and children of this community. They come into The Caribbean Service Center, present with the same issues or concerns, despite policy changes, despite our inability to provide all of the services they need. We thought creating more services and cycling funds is the best way we can help our clients. We have to show them that while the government cuts funds to help people like them, we [The Caribbean Service Center] care about them and their needs. We tell our clients that we are like them and they are like us. So, when other places turn them away, we find a way.

The Board also considered the strategy of offsetting organizational costs for operating programs to be a better alternative to instituting "fee for services." The Caribbean Service Center's leadership realized that if programs force clients to pay fees for services, it will discourage their working class, immigrant and racial-ethnic clients from seeking services.

A second solution or strategy used to overcome fiscal pressures was based on the decision to forge alliances with other organizations. Coalition building is considered by The Caribbean Service Center's Executive Director, Dr. Gary Whits, as the most effective means of coordinating its efforts with other agencies that are also committed to the goals of empowering and supporting racial-ethnic, Caribbean immigrant communities. According to Ferree and Hess (1994), Minkoff (1995), and Aldrich (1999), when faced with opportunities that may reduce the likelihood for co-optation and consequent changes in agenda setting, coalition building--as a more feasible option for community-based organization--allows organizations to deal with funding crises and expand its organizational niche. Recognizing this, Dr. Gary Whits believes that as long as The Caribbean Service Center has great access to the community and is strong in its ability to mobilize the community, the more power and control the organization has in its funding relationship with other agencies. Community leader, local activist, and supporter of The Caribbean Service Center, Rita David adds,

> We have to be careful. We want to have a better stream of funds and be able to work with organizations that are not totally dependent on grant renewals like we are--which is a good thing. But while working with these groups makes us a little more fiscally safe, we run the risk of them taking over. A merger-type relationship can create a situation where the group can use us, our access to the people, and before you know it, we lose our identity, we lose our focus. We would end up doing their work for them. So this is something that we have to be extremely careful about because these are some of the concerns any organization must consider when your group is fiscally caught up. We don't want The Caribbean Service Center to disappear as a result, that's all.

At the time of this research, The Caribbean Service Center worked very closely with "Central Hospital," also located in central Brooklyn. Central Hospital is mandated to meet and serve the needs of the broader Brooklyn community. These mandates are in the form of social policies and regulations that specify client groups, service eligibility requirements and services to be provided. Such policies and mandates bring fiscal support for implementing them. Central Hospital has more options for reaching the Caribbean population than The Caribbean Service Center has for funding sources. The Hospital can create special programs, hire special staff, or launch aggressive, outreach efforts, with money The Caribbean Service Center does not have access to. By working together, both organizations can reduce service duplication and increase their individual ability to reach their service population. In addition to managing this funding environment, The Caribbean Service Center attempts to create a diverse funding-base by forging relationships with other organizations in the community as a way to expand its access to money. Case Manager for the Asthma Program, LaShawna Minks explains,

> Many of our clients come through Central Hospital and are referred to us. It's important to have a good relationship with the Hospital. When a child or teenager has an asthma attack in the middle of the night and is taken to Central Hospital, I get called up because I am the case manager. I work with the attending physician to help the client. After the patient is discharged, I am the one, or my staff, that does the follow-up. We get a lot of support and can run programs or workshops through Central Hospital because they have more money than us. They give us supplies for patients when we do our outreach. We can't really afford that. You see, The Caribbean Service Center and the Hospital work hand in hand. We help them by taking on their patient-load and they help us by supporting our programs, providing supplies, and other assistance. It's like a marriage of sorts.

A smaller entity like The Caribbean Service Center, however, runs the risk of a larger entity such as Central Hospital having too much power over them. The Caribbean Service Center must ensure that its agenda and program priorities do not change. If this is a risk, The Caribbean Service Center must find new grantors and to a certain extent, tailor specific program projects to attract new funders and replace monies the organization has lost.

To date, Dr. Gary Whits and several Program Managers are confident that The Caribbean Service Center will remain autonomous in its mission, goals, and programming activities. Dr. Gary Whits, in particular, asserts that much of his work as the Executive Director requires him to continue to forge relationships with different types of service agencies, so that The Caribbean Service Center does not solely rely on the aid of organizations like Central Hospital. He contends that he is focused on maintaining the organization's fiscal sovereignty while finding resources that will help The Caribbean Service Center better serve its Caribbean immigrant community.

Efforts to ensure that the organization stays on task in its focus to support and provide services to Caribbean immigrants and other racial-ethnics in the central Brooklyn community are ongoing. At the same time, these efforts have been shaped by federal, state and local immigration policy mandates, which determine The Caribbean Service Center's ability to expand its programs and services over the last three decades. The Caribbean Service Center's interpretation of New York's immigration policy and the constraints such policies pose, through funding specifications or guidelines, impact the organization's decisions to offer certain programming that is believed would best benefit their Caribbean immigrant clients as well as a growing multiethnic Black community (including African Americans). Founders, Board, and staff members continually must respond to surges in service demands due to the expanding needs of its service community while adhering to policy mandates requiring organizations to embrace those that are culturally different.

In response to policy constraints, The Caribbean Service Center devised strategies, such as collaboratives, to diversify its programming and service provision. Also, because the founders, members of the Board and several community leaders are not only social service providers, but also are residents of the local Caribbean community, and in many instances, Caribbean immigrants, they interpret and internalize the implications of these policy changes. Their interpretation of these policies point to the legacies of race-based and immigrant-based government policies that impact the way racial-ethnic immigrants view their acceptance in American society.

As discussed earlier in this chapter, the United States has a history of restricting naturalization on the basis of race. America's pre-existing race and ethnic attitudes, ethnic group boundaries, and history of racial polarization and segregation coupled with immigration policies that determine which potential immigrants are desirable to admit and under what circumstances, are all factors that affect access to the opportunities available to racial-ethnic newcomers and the constraints they face. Racial-ethnic immigrants have faced stricter requirements to prove that their group has the desired characteristics for assimilability and government investment. Federal and state governments have required these immigrants to show whether they have the desired high technological skills or evidence of work experience, educational attainment, and/or language proficiencies.

This history, albeit America's legacy of race-based and immigrant-based government policies, affect institutions by regulating social programming, urban development, and the welfare state with specific provisions impacting racial-ethnic, immigrant groups full membership in society. Therefore, it is no surprise that founders' and members of the Board's interpretation of these policies has had a permanent affect on their views and determine the choices they made to develop culturally relevant services to support the advancement of Black Caribbeans.

Also, the founders' and members of the Board's interpretation of policies, I believe, impact clients' ability to gauge whether their status as immigrants and as Black people in the United States deems them "worthy" of receiving social services. Clients measure their worthiness or value on an organization's ability to overcome fiscal or policy constraints while remaining focused on protecting Caribbean people's interests and serving their needs.

In many ways, The Caribbean Service Center and its staff very consciously relay to clients that Caribbean immigrants and the larger Caribbean American community are important to the organization. As one of The Caribbean Service Center's board members, Lenroy Reynolds, stated earlier, "We tell our clients that we are like them and they are like us. So, when other places turn them away, we find a way." Hence, an underlying element of The Caribbean Service Center's strategies to expand its programming and to overcome fiscal obstacles is the promotion of Caribbean identity and its importance in the lives of the Caribbean community in central Brooklyn.

The Caribbean Service Center's connection to the community is more than offering culturally specific and targeted programming but also further emphasized through its ability to express and celebrate Caribbean identity and culture with its staff and clients. In many ways The Caribbean Service Center's internal organizational environment and the ways the organization's ideology, culture, and climate that foster Caribbean identity consciousness among its staff and ultimately impact its clients' understanding on the availability of Black Caribbean ethnic identity options.

CHAPTER 4

Homecoming: Celebrating Caribbean Ethnic Identity

Up to this point, I have described The Caribbean Service Center as: (1) a community-based organization, oriented for the people by the people of the community; (2) a grassroots movement, mobilized by a group of nurses who did not have direct control in local policy but had a stake in the outcome and viability of the Caribbean population; (3) a movement organization, having elements of action-oriented activities; (4) an institution, being a bureaucracy that is centralized, hierarchal with rules and procedures, and part of a larger social system of organizations that provide services; and to a certain degree, and (5) a NGO, because of its focus on maintaining a connection between the United States and Caribbean societies. The Caribbean Service Center has been all of these at different points of its history. The Caribbean Service Center's evolution is, however, not uncharacteristic of many ethnic-identified organizations.

Many ethnic-identified organizations have beginnings rooted in civic activity or mobilization, which bring people together who share similar and yet particular experiences, traditions, identities, struggles, and aspirations. Ethnic-identified organizations are community oriented, typically focused on building, improving, and sustaining the vitality of the racial-ethnic community it serves. According to Rosenstein (2006), these organizations tend to have mission statements and program activities that are clearly intended to preserve and promote

69

a specific community and its members. Whether their activities emphasize education and social services or arts and culture, ethnic-identified organizations offer a social space that link members of a racial-ethnic community together as well as provides a context where its members can develop and celebrate various social identities, including a racial and ethnic identity (see Rosenstein 2006).

Because of its name, history, and ability to provide a breadth of services for Caribbean immigrants and their families for over three decades, The Caribbean Service Center's founders, staff, and Board view the organization as a place where clients can feel welcomed and be comfortable to express who they are--ethnically, culturally, and linguistically. Yet, an organization's label as an ethnic-identified entity or its ability to provide a social and physical space for its ethnic target audience does not fully explain the role community-based organizations play in the ethnic identity assertions of its clients.

How does an ethnic-identified organization such as The Caribbean Service Center create a social space that provides a context where its members can celebrate Caribbean ethnicity? What organizational elements are present that influences their Caribbean immigrant clients' rate of adaptation, acculturation, and ultimately their ethnic identity assertions? Where does the sense of Caribbean identity come from? Who benefits from celebrating a Caribbean ethnic identity?

These questions are important because they get at the ways a community-based organization's internal polity can influence patterns of assimilation for its racial-ethnic, immigrant clients and the availability of ethnic identity options. Highlighting the significance of The Caribbean Service Center's ideology, climate, culture, and staff-client interaction involves examining how the organization's staff set the tone for how they unite, separate, and emphasize common bonds between themselves, their clients, and the community they serve. In this chapter, I consider how the founders' use of cultural symbols, to effectively dramatize grievances and demands of Caribbean immigrants informs the organization's ideology, culture, and climate and reinforces the sense of a Caribbean ethnicity and pride for both staff and clients. Also, The Caribbean Service Center's Caribbean ethnic identification, which involves promoting a sense of ethnic pride in its organizational programming activities, confirms to its Caribbean staff and clients that the organization has a cultural commitment to Caribbean immigrants that involves bringing diverse Caribbean people together, despite their intra-group distinctiveness.

Significance of Ethnic Identity in Organizations

According to identity theory, identities are self-cognitions that vary in their salience (likelihood of being invoked) based on a person's commitment (strength of ties) to a group or community of social relationships (Serpe and Stryker 1987). One of the central aspects of ethnic identity is a sense of commitment to one's ethnic group (Phinney 1991). Having a salient ethnic identity involves being committed to one's ethnic group, being proud of one's cultural heritage, and maintaining a strong sense of belonging to the ethnic community by participating in ethnic-designated organizations.

Ethnic identity is not a necessarily static self-concept. In fact, Caribbean immigrants' ethnic identity is strengthened during the acculturation process that allows Caribbean ethnic identity and American racial beliefs to co-exist, a context in which ethnic identity is more likely to persist (Phinney 1991). When Caribbean immigrants arrive in the United States, they learn that a Black racial status is assigned to them by the dominant group in society and that overcoming racial discrimination and stigmatization associated with a Black racial status can be difficult. It is this process that informs Caribbean immigrants and other racial-ethnic groups of the status-quo perceptions of Black identity. Many Caribbean immigrants choose to hold their own perceptions about their own ethnicity as a way to overcome the restrictions a Black racial identity poses in their ability to improve their socioeconomic and health conditions. Thus, utilizing and asserting ethnic identity options, such as a Caribbean ethnic identity, is often used as a strategy or coping source that buffers Caribbean immigrants from the stress of racial discrimination by preventing negative stereotypes associated with a Black racial status from affecting their self concept (Jackson and Lassiter 2001).

Community-based organizations support and enable clients to develop a strong sense of personal control and self-esteem, buffering or insulating them from the extreme stress of racial discrimination (Dion 1992). The construction of ethnic identity options is the result of a dialectical process involving an individual's self-identification and outsiders' ethnic designations of the individual (Jackson and Lassiter

2001). Since ethnicity changes situationally, the individual carries a portfolio of ethnic identities that are more or less salient in various situations and among various audiences. Espiritu (1992) and Padilla (1985, 1986) observe that individuals choose from an array of pan-ethnic and national-based identities depending on the perceived strategic utility and symbolic appropriateness of the identities in different settings and audiences.

The assertion of situational ethnicity or ethnic identity options is considered a benefit because it allows the individual to relate to a more heterogeneous community by using common elements of identity. Community leader, Shana Yugi, believes that this benefit is necessary for Caribbean immigrants because it increases their inclusiveness with other co-ethnics and with African Americans that live in the community. She goes on to add,

> It's not a flip-flop game at all; it's a way we all interact with one another. No one pretends to be something they're not but it's finding that common thing you have with someone and connecting with them--like the town or the school or the church you grew up in. It's that personal factor--like an experience--to relate to other people. The thing is, we all wear multiple hats but depending on who you are speaking to, you pull out that hat and start speaking like them. You hear the words they use, the things they speak about and then you say to yourself, 'yes, that's happened to me too.' Then you focus on that. So if you are a Trini then I relate to you as a Trini; if we are in a mixed group with other West Indians then I am West Indian too. I am all of those things but depending on where I am and who I am talking to, I may connect to people in that particular way.

Typically, ethnic-identified organizations like The Caribbean Service Center are developed and formed by ethnics who are united in some action against outside elements (such as changes in immigration policy or lack of culturally relevant services) that threaten the group's existence. By identifying with the plight of Caribbean immigrants in central Brooklyn, The Caribbean Service Center's founders utilize Caribbean ethnicity rather than an African American ethnic identity, leading to greater cohesiveness of a Caribbean community in central

Brooklyn. The Caribbean Service Center reinforced ethnic cohesiveness of the community through existing Caribbean community networks. The organization also expanded these networks by developing programming and attracting prospective staff workers and clients. For The Caribbean Service Center and its leaders, supporting Caribbean ethnicity is a way for the organization to petition the public (e.g., potential and current funders and politicians) to value the "special" needs (i.e., combined immigrant and racial-ethnic minority status) of Caribbean immigrants, and provide assistance to the Caribbean community. Leaders' interest that The Caribbean Service Center maintain its Caribbean cultural identity is rooted in their own emotional connection to and their positive value of Caribbean culture (see Hogg and Terry 2000; Tajfel 1974). In many regards, the leaders of The Caribbean Service Center established and promoted the notion that Caribbean immigrants are different from African Americans--by having special needs or concerns. Emphasizing a specific ethnic-focus--need or concern--enabled The Caribbean Service Center to carve out its own niche, providing culturally competent human services in a market that did not serve their client population effectively. While The Caribbean Service Center's emphasis on ethnicity is perceived positively by some Caribbean leaders in the community, it is important to consider that a latent consequence of promoting and supporting Caribbean ethnicity also serves to perpetuate key distinctions between Caribbean people and African Americans. One way in which The Caribbean Service Center promotes Caribbean cultural identity and in effect, influences the maintenance of a Caribbean ethnic identity of its staff and clients is through its organizational ideology, culture, and climate.

The Caribbean Service Center's Ideology, Culture, and Climate

The Caribbean Service Center's ability to connect with its Caribbean community members depends upon its ability to identify with their clients' experiences. Of the twenty The Caribbean Service Center founding and Board members, twelve are active. Many founding and current Board members shift roles within the organization's Board--some leave for a tenure of one to two years to work on other central Brooklyn community-related projects and then return to Board service.

During my interviews, many Board members and founders pointed to two factors that influenced their reasons for remaining involved with the organization as well as for recruiting new members to the Board: (1) sharing similar ethnic composition and cultural consciousness of the organization's client population and understanding community members' everyday experiences, and (2) sharing the belief that many of the needs of the Caribbean community are still unmet. In effect, these two factors serve as the underlying basis for The Caribbean Service Center's ideology, culture, and climate.

One way in which organizations identify with their constituency is through creating an organizational climate that reflects its constituency's ideological beliefs (McGregor 1960). The Caribbean Service Center's founders' and leaders' ideological beliefs inform its director's leadership style. The Caribbean Service Center's director must think and act politically, be able to communicate effectively, share information strategically, and create influence networks necessary to increase positive social, economic, and political consequences for the organization as well as solidify its bond with the Caribbean community. The Caribbean Service Center's current Executive Director, Dr. Gary Whits's, leadership style is one that was described by Board member Maria Hernandez as,

....a true Caribbean man--stubborn, a bit direct, and demanding but can be very charismatic at times. [laughs] I would say, fights for his Caribbean people.... [Dr. Gary Whits] has very specific immediate goals for us to meet as an organization but he wants us all to strive to achieve the goal of empowering our people and better serving them. So far, I think he is an effective leader and co-worker.

As Maria Hernandez described, Dr. Gary Whits' leadership style embodied masculine personality traits stereotypically associated with Caribbean men. Dr. Gary Whits's leadership style reflects a gender dynamic that is socially acceptable in Caribbean culture. Accordingly, it is believed that Caribbean men in high status positions should adhere to ideals of masculine behavior—strong-minded, driven, and charismatic. Dr. Gary Whits's leadership style reflects traditional cultural ideals that exist within Caribbean culture, with which Caribbean people readily can identify. In this regard, his leadership style does not hinder the organization's ability to work effectively with mainstream funding agencies or with The Caribbean Service Center's predominantly female, Caribbean staff members. According to this Board member, Dr. Gary Whits's leadership style helped confirm to the public that The Caribbean Service Center is a Caribbean-identified organization in the community.

Together, an organization's ideology (beliefs and vision) and a director's leadership style creates and establishes an organization's culture and climate for staff members and clients to identify with and participate in. The climate of an organization is learned by its members (McGregor 1960). Staff members and clients make inferences about the organization through the policies, practices, procedures, and routines that they are subject to and on the kinds of behaviors that are expected and that get rewarded. The organization's staff members' and clients' beliefs and values constitute the organization's culture. An organization's culture concerns the less conscious but firmly implanted beliefs and values staff members have of the organization. While the organization's climate (policies and practices) are observable, the beliefs and values are not so directly visible.

Staff's values and beliefs (culture) influence their interpretations of organizational policies, practices, and procedures (climate). Organizational values inform how staff members view their roles in the organization and shape how staff members relate to their clients, identify with their concerns, and assist them (see Schneider, Brief, and Guzzo 1995). Also, clients make inferences about the organization's climate and culture. Clients learn from their interaction with staff members about the organization's culture and climate and whether the organization is one that supports and strongly identifies with them and the rest of the community. Lashawna Minks, a case manager for the Asthma Program adds,

> I think that we know firsthand as immigrants that immigrants have specific needs or certain barriers so we do try to tailor it. So that's like a cultural thing. We have an understanding of these feelings and ideas and can best help our clients. We try to find the appropriate support for them. We know they are confident in us because they show up and want me and my staff to help.

The Caribbean Service Center's external polities (e.g., federal and state policies and funding opportunities) aided in its expansion of services and helped shape its specific programmatic goals while reaffirming its organizational existence and role in the larger community context. Even as The Caribbean Service Center faced external polity changes or pressures, its internal polity (culture, climate, and ideology) did not change; instead, its internal polity--which focuses on improving the Caribbean community--became more defined. In this regard, The Caribbean Service Center's internal polity impacts staff engagement and interaction with clients and their efforts in shaping immigrant clients' attitudes, perceptions, and/or behaviors, including ethnic identity options. Therefore, The Caribbean Service Center's culture and climate suggest to staff and clients that its activities are to support Caribbean immigrants and better serve them. As a result, clients believe in The Caribbean Service Center and utilize its services. The Caribbean Service Center's ability to connect with its Caribbean community members is based on the organization consistently and publicly affirming its commitment to the community by asserting that it is a community-based organization for Caribbean people, created by Caribbean people, located in the Caribbean community that offers various programming initiatives for the betterment of Caribbean people.

Staff Identities, Staff-Client Interactions and Celebrating Caribbean Ethnicity

In his book The Presentation of Self in Everyday Life, Erving Goffman (1959) used a cognitive approach to understand interpersonal interactions. He examined how information is disseminated and how information is received. Goffman argued that we influence what others think of us by projecting certain cues about ourselves. Others then define us based on their experiences and stereotypic expectations of our behavior. In essence, Goffman identified how "self" is projected and received by others. Ethnic identity is a part of that self. Ethnic symbols and shared perceptions include negative and positive stereotypes of ethnic groups (White and Burke 1987). Positive stereotypes, according to Eames and Goode (1977), can produce cohesion and can be used as symbols of shared meanings. Individuals internalize the meanings or positive stereotypes that are associated with an ethnic group and based on these shared definitions make possible a strong sense of ethnic identity (see Mackie and Brinkerohoff 1984; Obidinski 1978).

Many of The Caribbean Service Center's staff members identify as Caribbean and recognize that others also identify them as Caribbean. Within an organization whose staff members are 85 % Caribbean (1st generation and 1.5 generation immigrants) and whose Caribbean clients represent 85 % of the total client population, the interactions between staff and staff-clients reinforce internalized shared meanings and symbols of "Blackness," Caribbean culture and ethnicity. A former program manager and current Board member, Martha Espinosa, gives an example,

> I identify myself as Black Hispanic. That's it. I don't go any further because I look at it from my skin color, its dark. Caribbean people look at race in terms of color and even culture. I am a dark woman, so I'm Black. [My grandparents] were from Jamaica. My parents were born in Panama but grew up speaking English. My parents spoke English to me and my siblings. I spoke English at home and learned about Caribbean culture at home. Now, I was born in a Spanish-speaking country. I went to school and all my education is in Spanish. So, because Panama is a Spanish country, I identify myself as a Black Hispanic. Yet, everything changes here [America].

Participants, such as Martha, expressed a conception of "Blackness" that emphasizes blending language, culture, and nation-state identity with physical appearance (i.e., skin tone), which is different from America's monolithic indication of racial membership. Different from the United States, many countries in the Caribbean established no systematic discrimination-type Jim Crow laws post-abolition and instead, emphasized a state-led nationalism that is intended to be more inclusive of the cultural, linguistic, and racial-ethnic diversity (albeit African, European, and Indigenous Indian) and history of its people. Arguably, it is this type of racial democracy, which many Caribbean nations utilize to shape national loyalty and promote civil obedience, informs Caribbean people's understanding that a more flexible and inclusive racial order encourages unity, reduces division, and promotes shared interest for nation-building and positive

assertions of all citizen's political, economic and social rights. This is
not to say that informal discrimination by skin tone (light versus darker
skinned) and class (elite versus egalitarian) is not evident in these
nations, however, it is clear that for participants, the special importance
of exploring and identifying with a specific national, ethnic, and
cultural heritage is critical to their own self-concept and meaning of
Blackness.

Equally as important to participants is the sense of commonality of
experience that is shared by other Caribbean people when they arrive to
the United States and face the daily challenges of overcoming rigid
American concepts of race and Blackness. Martha Espinosa goes on to
add,

> I will be very honest, I have no problems now when somebody
> will say, "Are you a West Indian?   Are you from the
> Caribbean?" I use to get very upset because Caribbean or
> West Indian used to have a negative connotation.   People
> called us "boat people" or "coconuts." Because of that I used
> to say, right away, I am not a West Indian. I am not from the
> Caribbean.   I would say, "I'm from Panama which is in
> Central America and that is a Hispanic country."   But I've
> learned to come to terms that my ancestors are Black and from
> the Caribbean. We are all brown people; some darker than
> others. We eat the same foods, listen to the same music, and
> have the same experiences when we come to America. Here,
> we're all seen as Black people. It does not matter whether you
> speak Spanish, French, or English, once you have color, a
> broad nose, and so, we're Black. So it doesn't even matter
> anymore if people call us, "coconuts" or "boat people." I am a
> Caribbean but I am also a Black person. I am Black--which is
> different from African American--and I'm proud and
> comfortable with being Black. But I've come a long way.

This definition of "Blackness" and its social meaning for
Caribbean people in America raises a paradox that reflects the
distinction participants often made between their individual self-
concept and identity and the political meaning of being Black in
America. The racial democracy experienced by participants from their
Caribbean country of origin made it possible for them to embrace and

celebrate aspects of their racial-ethnic culture openly without being impacted by overt antagonistic racial exclusion. Yet, upon their arrival to the United States, many of the Caribbean participants realized they could not benefit from this ideological concept of inclusiveness since racial exclusion, racially distinct legal treatments, and ethnic conflict is the basis for American social order and hierarchy.

For many staff members, they internalized the meaning of skin color and the negative stereotypes that are associated with African Americans and constructed a rationale that defines how Caribbean are (or not) included in an African American community. Some staff members emphasized the sentiment that there are differences between Caribbean people and African Americans. Other staff members assert that they share similar African ancestry with African Americans in the United States but were adamant that they were a different type of Black people. Many staff members want to be viewed by society as Caribbean, an ethnic identity which encompasses "a focus on achievement, pride in African ancestry, and some conservative values" in fear of being stigmatized as lazy and in an attempt to overcome racial discrimination (Vickerman 1999: 139). In making these distinctions, staff members put as much distance as possible between themselves and African Americans by maintaining a strong sense of Caribbean ethnic identity. Robert Lawson, a youth outreach worker for the Youth Services Program, takes this point,

> Look, I see it all the time and it isn't right. Me and my family are immigrants--although I've been here so long I'm more American than West Indian. I grew up around here, went to school, and had a lot of Black [American] friends growing up. When I was younger, my mom used to be scared about the guys I used to hang with and she would say ignorant things like "they're a bunch of crabs in a barrel." I mean, real messed up stuff like that. I didn't understand her until I would go on interviews for a job or internship and the recruiter would look at my last name and ask where I was from. I'd start talking about my family, places we'd go--yeah, yeah, whatever. Then, the interview would take a different tone. The approach would be different, like the recruiter was surprised and intrigued all at the same time. So, imagine that. I've always tried to blend in and be like my boys in school and on the

block. I wasn't trying to be different-- because who wants to be different? I had my run-ins with guys that wanted to jump me because my family isn't from here. Then, when I would go on interviews, I'd be the West Indian young guy--the hard working interesting cat, meaning, I wasn't like the rest. Many times, I got the job or the internship over my boys. And that's when it clicked for me. That was my edge, my advantage. So, it isn't right but this is America. You've got to use what you got to get what you want [chuckle]. I mean, the deal is, it's all about the slice of the pie. Who wouldn't want a slice as opposed to a crumb? You tell me....

Because a large proportion of The Caribbean Service Center's staff members are Caribbean born, their racial and ethnic similarities foster close interactions. The Caribbean Service Center's staff members convey powerful psychological messages to their clients that concern self image, stigma, and about the realities of race since they already have the inside knowledge about the destiny of racial-ethnic groups in America. Etzioni (1964) suggests that a close relationship between staff leads to sensitivity to the client, which in turn leads to the clients' responsiveness to services. At The Caribbean Service Center, race and ethnicity become a factor that advances rather than impedes the service delivery process. As a member of the Caribbean ethnic group, the staff member does not have to be convinced of or lectured to about the destiny of Caribbean people in America.

Caribbean clients' responsiveness to The Caribbean Service Center's staff and Caribbean-centered services are related to clients' confidence in staff members' sensitivity to their needs. For example, multicultural specialists Herring (1996), Locke (1997), and White and Parham (1990), based on their observed treatment of African Americans in America (i.e., a history of racial discrimination, and America's reaction to darker skin tones), have argued that racial-ethnic immigrant clients lack confidence in the counseling or assistance given to them by non- racial-ethnic immigrants. Caribbean clients do not trust non-ethnic service providers. The lack of trust that can exist in these circumstances often leads to client guardedness and the inability of staff and clients to establish a rapport. The Caribbean Service Center's staff and clients are already more likely to adhere to similar world values, meanings, and processes. As members of the same ethnic group, the staff member and client may share the commonality of history, background, experience and world view. Tiffany Wells, a case manager for the Youth Services Program adds,

> I am proud to be a West Indian. It's no lie when you speak with me. But I try not to push that pride onto others. Although, I do find that when my proudness comes up in casual conversations in the halls, clients are drawn to it. They love it and identify with it.

Language patterns (i.e., use of patois, a dialect that combines broken English, French, and Spanish languages) connote a unity with and familiarity to the client that translates into the client's feeling comfortable and open to receiving staff feedback. In speaking patois with staff members, clients learn that Caribbean ethnicities are accepted. Veronica Stanley, a staff member for the Maternal Health and WIC programs, describes the lack of trust experienced by Caribbean clients between themselves and a non-Caribbean provider is also felt by the few African Americans that work at and receive services through The Caribbean Service Center. She goes on to say,

> It is hard for African Americans to come here and feel included and comfortable all of the time. Some of my African American clients and even some staff are a bit put off at first by Caribbean clients who are loud and always speaking patois. Some say it's like "they" [Caribbean people] are taking over. Other clients have questioned me, wanting to know if they are really getting the "real deal" here. I say to them, "We don't discriminate; we employ and serve everyone, even whites and Asians. But even after saying all of this, I can see how African Americans would be skeptical about the information and care [they receive]. We always have something going on that supports some type of Caribbean or Caribbean American alliance or activity. These things are broad enough to apply to all Blacks, even African Americans, but I think, like I said, people are put off sometimes.

Organizational Elements that Influence Client's Caribbean Identity

While the common thread of ethnic group experience allows The Caribbean Service Center's staff to be aware of and address community concerns, The Caribbean Service Center also is able to maintain a strong, ethnic affiliation with the Caribbean community by hiring former clients as staff members or using clients as volunteers. Hiring former clients confirms the organization's reputation in the community as a place that supports Caribbean people. Victoria Samms, a general case manager and outreach worker elaborates,

> We [The Caribbean Service Center] have a relationship with the community. It's about empowerment, partnership. Community members can feel a sense of ownership. We create this sense of unity. Don't get me wrong, every work place has issues, difficult personalities, but for the most part, we are able to create this sense of unity among Caribbean people. We hire individuals that share the same focus as our agenda, we hire past clients. I was a former client. Now I am a case manager and I do some outreach. I use my personal experiences to help others. If people disrespect you in an outside agency because you're Caribbean, I tell you to say that you're Black. That's worked for me. It's worked for many of us. And vice versa. When I am not working and people see me in the market, they say that I am successful and they want to be like me. They want to know how I got services here and why did some other agency turn me away. I tell them; it's real to them, because they see it work in my life. It's like a personal testimony.

Another way The Caribbean Service Center's staff members convey powerful messages to their Caribbean clients that concern the realities of race and ethnicity in America is by sharing information about the larger society and, more specifically, how to negotiate the social service system.

The program manager for Legal Services, Wanda Martines explains,

> Well, let's face it. People treat people differently. I know this
> first hand being an immigrant myself. People automatically
> treat me differently if they see me as Black [American] or
> Caribbean. If people knew I was Caribbean they would think
> there was a language barrier because of my accent and assume
> I was stupid. Funny, I speak English and have a JD! So, when
> Caribbean and/or other immigrant clients come in here and say
> that their child's school says their son or daughter is
> consistently misdiagnosed as having learning deficits because
> the child has a very thick accent--I advise them as to what to
> do... I know how to best help them--legally--within the
> system that oftentimes discriminates against them, and they
> listen.

When the staff conveys integral information about "the system,"
they alert clients to alternatives available to them and strategies they
need to get additional services under the current public assistance
system. Most clients learn to trust the staff members' advice. Staff
members also teach their Caribbean immigrant clients how to get best
results from other social service and health organizations (i.e., clinics,
WIC centers, and Immigration programs). They teach and prepare
clients how to work with other agencies in order to obtain favorable
treatment.

Providing information becomes one of the ways staff members
support their Caribbean clients. Staff members construct a connection
between themselves and the client. In the case of The Caribbean
Service Center, ethnicity tends to be the basis of clients' trust of staff.
LaShawna Minks, case manager for the Asthma Program explains,

> I think that we know firsthand as immigrants that immigrants
> have specific needs or certain needs or certain barriers so we
> do try to tailor it. For example, we had one case where it was
> someone from Haiti and she just didn't believe in doctors
> because her grandmother was a Voodoo priest and she
> provided all the care that she would ever need. So that's like a
> cultural thing. Because many of us are Caribbean people, we

have an understanding of these feelings and ideas and can best
help our clients. We try to find the appropriate support for
them.

Even under circumstances where clients interact with multiple staff
members that are from different Caribbean countries, clients still feel
connected to the organization's Caribbean culture and identity.
While it must be noted that there are intra-ethnic distinctions
among Caribbeans that are island-specific (e.g., selection of physical,
psychological, emotional or social attributes of that particular island
that Caribbean people identify and celebrate), Caribbean identity is a
more salient factor than an island-specific, gender or class identity. For
example, on one occasion, during a community meeting, a working
class Bajan couple complained that middle-class Caribbeans did not
understand the couple's working class plight in the United States, and
wanted community members to be more informed about the issues that
affect working class immigrants. At that point, a self-identified middle
class Antiguan man, who had been in the United States for almost a
decade, agreed but wanted the community to add a few other concerns
to the public agenda for Caribbean community members. The ensuing
debate turned to focus on issues that affect all islanders, including those
of various class and religious backgrounds.

The general experiences of Caribbeans dealing with racism,
discrimination, poverty, and access to better health care and education
became points that the Bajan couple and the Antiguan man could agree
on. Island nationalities were heightened when individuals focused on
the politics and circumstances of their particular homeland, including
the ideological concept of unity and inclusivity as supported by similar
nation-state identities and notions of racial democracy. Also, clients'
sense of Caribbeanness--as a regional identity is heightened when
island nationals share similar experiences in America. The various
cultural and social characteristic differences that exist across islands do
not seem to affect Caribbeans willingness to be ethnically grouped
together and identify as Caribbean in America. "Caribbeanness" is the
salient factor that strengthens the existence of a Caribbean identity in
the community by staff and clients of The Caribbean Service Center.
Caribbean identity has significant implications on the interaction
between Caribbeans and African Americans.

Promoting a Sense of Ethnic Pride

The development and the assertion of a Caribbean ethnic identity is the result of certain structural features of urban immigrant life, including the presence of ethnic-designated community organizations like The Caribbean Service Center (see Yancey 1976). Moore (1990) suggests that among Caribbean immigrants there is a growing need for a collective common identification. This need arises out of the central role race has in determining the life chances and social positions of Black ethnics (Padilla 1986). Caribbean immigrants share structural commonalities and the imposition of racial and ethnic labels (Espiritu, 1990). Caribbean immigrants then find their social position within the limits of the dominant racial symbolic system--a system that assigns them negative characteristics--by developing and connecting to ethnic-based organizations, networks, and communities.

At The Caribbean Service Center, Caribbean immigrants use the option of affirming and promoting Caribbean ethnic pride because it gives them an opportunity to overcome the power of others to impose their identity definitions. In this regard, The Caribbean Service Center's organizational setting, within a diverse Black community, makes race-ethnic identity very important. Promoting Caribbean ethnic pride emerges, interestingly, in contrast and comparison to meanings of other racial-ethnic identities (i.e., African American). The Caribbean Service Center internally supports Caribbean identity and culture through its organizational ideology, staff-client relations, and programming, yet its setting in an ethnically heterogeneous community makes ethnicity more salient. According to Burke (1980), racial-ethnic identity is more important to individuals when they are in a setting where they encounter members of other ethnic groups. It is in this context, I suggest that the "I-we relationship" is critical to understanding what a Caribbean identity is and who benefits from asserting a Caribbean ethnicity.

As I mentioned earlier, Goffman's (1959) approach to understanding interpersonal interactions identifies how one's identity or "self" is projected and received by others. Inherent in this explanation is the notion that individuals have the desire to understand others and expect others to understand them. In doing so, individuals find similarities and distinguish themselves by the presence of others. In effect, individuals develop the notion that there is no 'I' without the existence of 'you' when defining and expressing identity consciousness (see Yu and Kwan 2008). When the perception of those that are initially perceived as an "other" are perceived as similar to or like oneself, then the "I" is expanded into a "we" relationship in a common environment. Hence, individuals categorize the "we" as in-group and others/"they" as out-group.

In urban Black communities like central Brooklyn where resources and culturally competent and relevant services are scarce for both Caribbean immigrants and African Americans, there are heightened tensions in part due to this "I-we relationship." Nagel's (1986) competition theory would suggest that Caribbean immigrants and their promotion of Caribbean identity consciousness reinforce competition or conflict between themselves (the "I" or the in group) and African Americans (the "they" or out group) over resources available to both groups. Despite the implications of the tensions, which arise as a result of Caribbean ethnic identification, Caribbean identity is important and meaningful as promoting Caribbeanness in the lives of The Caribbean Service Center's Caribbean immigrant clients and staff because of the sense of solidarity of immigrant ethnic experiences that binds them together.

Implications of Supporting Clients' Caribbean Ethnic Identity Distinctiveness

With its high degree of Caribbean ethnic identity consciousness, The Caribbean Service Center responds to an urban environment in which there is a great deal of ethnic heterogeneity and complexity. Here, this ethnic-identified organization's strong ethnic commitment to Caribbeans acts as a buffer in an environment that fosters discrimination against those who are labeled African American. The organization is intended to support its service community and alleviate the stress caused by racism, racial tension and conflict by providing a safe haven where members can identify with a group of people like themselves.

When staff members share information with clients regarding where to go for additional services and advise them (whether through an anecdote or direct advice) to assert a Caribbean identity, they are teaching clients to use their ethnicity to obtain maximum advantage. Many staff members admitted to purposefully encouraging and advising their clients to assert an ethnicity that will give them the greatest benefits. In this regard The Caribbean Service Center sanctions the development of a Caribbean collectivity when its staff members share information with clients about differences in access to referral services when a Caribbean ethnic identity, a Black identity, or an African American ethnic identity is asserted in various situations. The similarity of experience and the process of information exchange affirms the "we" aspect of the "I-we relationship." When explicitly advising their clients to assert a Caribbean ethnic identity, these staff members indirectly assist Caribbean immigrant clients in making distinctions between themselves and African Americans. In making these distinctions, Caribbean staff members and clients reify dominant racial ideologies learned before and after their arrival to America.

When I had the opportunity to interact, informally, with The Caribbean Service Center's clients, many shared with me that they learned from staff members and other clients that the ethnic identity "African American" carried with it negative associations (e.g., being lazy, untrustworthy). Many of The Caribbean Service Center's clients believed that in order to achieve "success," they had to internalize the stereotype that Caribbean people are different from African Americans-- Caribbeans are hard working, reliable, and adept businesspeople. Because The Caribbean Service Center supports and its staff celebrates Caribbean identity, Caribbeans express positive feelings about Caribbean ethnicity that leads clients to ask: "Why should I feel ashamed of who and what I am?" (See Sue and Sue 1990 Racial/Cultural Identity Development Model (R/CID). By holding positive sentiments towards Caribbean people, The Caribbean Service Center's Caribbean immigrant clients do not fully assimilate into the African American population. Staff members, indirectly, encourage their Caribbean immigrant clients to reject negative stereotypes associated with African Americans by divorcing themselves from identifying with African American identity while celebrating Caribbean ethnicity. This was particularly true for staff members that served clients who conveyed a sense of Caribbean cultural authenticity that deemed them closer to the culture--those that spoke the language or dialect, visited their country or origin often, maintained social and economic ties to the Caribbean, and had recently immigrated.

By no means do I believe that The Caribbean Service Center's promotion of ethnic differentiation is intended to be malicious toward African Americans. In fact, I believe that because The Caribbean Service Center has African American staff members, board members and participating community leaders, and African American, Asian, and European clients, the organization does not purposefully discriminate or alienate African Americans or non-Caribbeans from its services or from participating in its community efforts. Yet, by promoting ethnic distinctions, though unintentional, The Caribbean Service Center also facilitates the reification of African American's low social status.

Staff members recognize the larger social implications of ethnic distinctions that exist between Caribbean immigrants and African Americans. As a result, Dr. Gary Whits focuses on The Caribbean Service Center's need to simplify and reduce differentiation by increasing programming support and hiring more African Americans. Yet, on a staff-client level, staff members reported that Caribbean clients are at times apprehensive to confide in non-Caribbean staff members because clients believe that African American case managers do not understand their dual plight as racial-ethnics and as immigrants. A case manager for the Domestic Violence Program, Sarah Flynn asserts that,

> Some clients come in here to speak with me about certain topics because they know I am from [their country]. I can understand their perspective and their level of comfort, however, I know that if some of the other case managers, who are, let's say African American speak with such clients, [clients] will not disclose as much information or even trust them fully because they think African Americans are somewhat insensitive to their special needs or concerns. In general, I think it is this [lack of trust] that creates tension between African Americans and Caribbean people.

The lack of trust that exists between Caribbeans and African Americans is based on the stereotype that African Americans do not have the same cultural values as Caribbean people when it comes to education, family life, upbringing of children, and work ethic (Waters, 1999). Stereotypical sentiments toward African Americans are not one-sided. Indeed, African Americans also hold stereotypes against Caribbeans in the community. Veronica Stanley works at one of the satellite locations of The Caribbean Service Center, which serves the largest proportion of African American clients The Caribbean Service Center has (approximately 10%). She suggests that African Americans are confused by Caribbean people and their assertion of an island-specific or Caribbean identity. She argues that African Americans believe that Caribbeans deny their racial identity and believe that they are superior to African Americans. Veronica adds,

> From what I understand from my African-American clients and staff members is that there is resentment particularly from the African-American community towards Caribbean people. Some African Americans believe that Caribbean immigrants come here, take their jobs, their men, and do nothing to contribute to the cause for Black people. This attitude makes it hard for us here [at The Caribbean Service Center] to prove to African Americans that these are simply stereotypes. You see, African Americans see the name of the organization and think we only serve women or Caribbeans only and not them. We have that double duty of trying to explain that we are here for everyone and it's just that the organization was started by a group of women from the Caribbean. After that, it is up to the client to trust that the organization can and will provide them with proper services.

The stereotypes that exist between Caribbeans and African Americans not only exacerbate tensions but also fuel ethnic distinctiveness. In the central Brooklyn community where African Americans and Caribbeans live in close proximity to one another, ethnic distinctiveness and ethnic celebration creates competition between both groups that only helps to perpetuate the inequalities and the disparities (e.g., race, health and education) that exists.

As an ethnic-identified organization, The Caribbean Service Center provides a source of information, services, and communication useful to the survival of many Caribbean immigrants in central Brooklyn. The Caribbean Service Center contributes to the social development of Caribbean communities in that it creates some equilibrium, attempting to keep various degrees of ostracism from becoming total isolation.

The Caribbean Service Center's leaders and staff members see their responsibility and duty as improving standards of living and health for fellow Caribbeans, and attaining a level of success in their own organizational operations.

In an atmosphere of racial discrimination and lack of culturally relevant services, The Caribbean Service Center serves as more than a place of accessing and utilizing services; it is a home. The stories staff members, the Board, and volunteers told of their experiences in serving Caribbean ethnics was often described as a homecoming, a social space where Caribbean people and their families feel comfortable. For most of my participants, home is a symbol of refuge or acceptance and of comfort; it is a social and physical space where individuals gain a sense of understanding about who they are, racial and ethnically. The Caribbean Service Center is the physical space that has helped to sustain a sense of Caribbean identity consciousness for its staff, Board, and clients, including community members.

The Caribbean Service Center provides avenues for the positive development of individual ethnic identity and Caribbean immigrant public images. The Caribbean Service Center fulfills many of the social and psychological needs of its Caribbean clients in the community by supporting Caribbean culture and ethnicity. Its staff members use their connection and affinity towards Caribbean culture as a way to create a favorable impression with clients. Their Caribbean clients view the organization and its staff as credible (expert and trustworthy) and capable of handling their specific needs and issues. Credibility makes The Caribbean Service Center attractive, thus allowing the organization to have greater influence over their Caribbean clients' conception of race and identity.

At the same time, developing, sustaining, and asserting Caribbean identity consciousness is also predicated on a set of shared understandings of America's definition of Blackness. The Caribbean Service Center's promotion of a Caribbean consciousness, through its ideology, culture, and climate, provides a setting by which its staff and clients are able to celebrate their own Caribbean ethnicity as an alternative to an African American identity. Within this context, Caribbean people can interpret and internalize the varied and possibly contradictory information they learn as clients about race and ethnic identity in America. Having this space is critical to understanding how

Caribbean immigrants develop identity strategies to adjust to racial and ethnic oppressions that exist in the larger society. While having a social and physical space has proved to be a positive resource to staff and members of central Brooklyn's Caribbean community, the existence of such an organization impacts its Caribbean immigrant clients' segmented assimilation paths and their rates of assimilation. The promotion and celebration of Caribbean ethnicity slows the rate of traditional immigrant incorporation (i.e., contact, competition, accommodation, and assimilation) because many immigrants *choose* to hold on to island traditions and maintain a Caribbean identity consciousness.

By identifying with and asserting a Caribbean ethnic identity, Caribbean immigrants and their families experience assimilation along different pathways--segmented assimilation. These immigrants' participation in organizations like The Caribbean Service Center speeds up the rate by which they internalize the norms and values of American society including their understanding of race and identity, and the facilitation and utilization of Black Caribbean ethnic identity options. For many of the founders, Board, and staff of The Caribbean Service Center, asserting a pan-ethnic Black identity, which also includes Caribbean ethnicity, has led to their relative upward mobility (i.e., homeownership, semi and professional occupations, and professional degrees) (see Piedra and Engstrom 2009). Participants' connection to a very tight-knit Caribbean immigrant community has served to solidify their sense of Caribbean collectivity and solidarity, which ultimately goaded them to mobilize around Caribbean immigrant concerns and later establish The Caribbean Service Center.

Conversations with participants show that the assertion of Black Caribbean ethnic identity options is a challenging experience that requires ongoing negotiations of conflicting messages of "what it means to be Black" coming from mainstream American definitions (e.g., being African American) and co-ethnic social settings. In asserting Black Caribbean ethnic identity options, Caribbean immigrants construct a broader sense of Black pan-ethnic identity by conjuring and utilizing the same symbols of racial pride (i.e., celebrating African culture and customs, and highlighting diversity of language, skin tone, and hair texture) used by African Americans. At the same time, participants often distanced themselves from negative stereotypes by employing different and more positive meanings associated with a Black racial identity that diverge from mainstream understandings of race.

The irony here is that it is difficult to challenge American mainstream notions of race by using the same Black racial symbols to assert specific Caribbean ethnic identity that is also used to denigrate native-born Blacks. Yet, utilizing Black racial symbols in asserting Black Caribbean ethnic identity does not always incite racial solidarity between African Americans and Caribbean immigrants. In fact, celebrating Caribbean ethnic distinctiveness can incite tension. In a community where it is critical to reduce inter-group conflict in order to build and empower its people, one question remains unanswered: at what cost does promoting and maintaining Caribbean ethnicity has on the overall Black community of central Brooklyn?

CHAPTER 5

Problems and Possibilities

"Up! You mighty race, you can accomplish what you will."

--Marcus Mosiah Garvey

As an ethnic-identified organization, The Caribbean Service Center is responsible for bridging the gap between their Caribbean immigrant clients' pre-migration knowledge about America and their American reality. The Caribbean Service Center seeks to support immigrants and their families by helping them: (1) see the value of understanding the "race game," and (2) navigate through race-based systems of bureaucracy (see works by Stepick, Rey, and Mahler 2009; Rong and Brown 2002). The organization also provides their immigrant clients and community members the opportunity to celebrate Caribbean culture, and develop and assert Black Caribbean ethnic identity options. In particular, the organization's ability to support and celebrate Caribbean culture and identity is seen in its respect for varied socio-cultural orientations of its clients, its diverse cultural foundation, and its programming which highlights the cultural and psychological strengths of immigrants and the existing bicultural resources present in the community.

As a community-based organization, The Caribbean Service Center is also responsible for improving the overall well-being of the broader Black community it serves. The organization is charged with strategically developing various approaches to help connect both Caribbean immigrant clients and the central Brooklyn African American community to economic opportunities and social services.

93

To do so, practitioners must broadly identify shared themes across inter-group divide and learn and understand important cultural, social, and linguistic variations within the broader Black racial-ethnic community.

Today, The Caribbean Service Center, along with many community leaders, social workers, and health professionals in central Brooklyn are renewing their efforts to reduce the increasing rates of unemployment, homelessness, domestic violence, AIDS/HIV, and infant mortality that plague central Brooklyn's Black community. Indeed, The Caribbean Service Center's community leaders, Board, and staff conclude that increasing political participation of community members is one of many important steps for more equitable distribution of resources and better provisions of services. They believe that members of this diverse Black, immigrant community must have political strength to gain bargaining power to fight for better social programs and policies.

As noted in Chapter Three, The Caribbean Service Center's ability to gain political strength via political participation affects its ability to petition for more resources. According to resource mobilization theorists (Emerson 1962; Zald 1970) community-based organizations like The Caribbean Service Center must engage in more explicit political approaches (i.e., mobilizing their clients and establishing political alliances) to gain the attention and support of funders. In the case of central Brooklyn, while Caribbean immigration continues to increase steadily, their political clout is not proportionate to their size. According to a 2000 New York City Census report, both Caribbean immigrants and African Americans in central Brooklyn lack the political strength needed to gain bargaining power with politicians. The lack of the Black community's political strength is reflected in the group's dismal voter participation rates, political visibility, and overall apathy. This lack of political strength ultimately impedes The Caribbean Service Center's efforts in the community revitalization process.

In this chapter I argue two critical points. First, I argue that The Caribbean Service Center faces the difficult task of providing services to central Brooklyn's Black community--including both Caribbean immigrants and African Americans. Because The Caribbean Service Center has the reputation of being a Caribbean-identified organization, the organization inevitably contributes to inter-group tensions that already exist between Caribbean immigrants and African Americans. Second, I argue that the racial and ethnic tensions that persist, particularly ethnic differentiation between Caribbeans and African Americans, contribute to the Black community's (including both American and foreign-born Blacks) growing community disintegration, apathy, and transnationalism. I identify some of the consequences that arise as a result of these tensions by considering the following two questions: Do Caribbean immigrants and African Americans, despite their ethnic distinctiveness, share a common set of racial group interests; and is it possible (or enough) for these two Black ethnic groups to unify over a common Black agenda?

Understanding today's ethnic tensions between Caribbean immigrants and African Americans

The ethnic tensions that persist today between Caribbean immigrants and African Americans did not always exist. Caribbean immigrants and African Americans indeed have a history in developing strong Black identity and group consciousness. This history goes as far back as at the turn of the 20th century when New York City experienced a heavy influx of Caribbean migration and African American migration from the South. A precondition for the construction of group identity and consciousness amongst African Americans and Caribbean immigrants during this time was the centrality of race or the concept of "Blackness."

Group identities are constructed internally when individuals' awareness of belonging to a racial group and having an attachment to that group is based on the perception of having shared beliefs, feelings, interests, and ideas (McClain et al 2009). In addition, group identities are also "constructed externally by communication within and between the involved groups, and they are as much concerned with the process of being identified as they are with making identifications" (Mana, Orr, and Mana 2009: 450-451). In a country like the United States, race or the concept of Blackness is a complex template for representing and organizing social knowledge, constructing sameness and difference, and making sense of everyday actions (Brubaker 2009). Because race is complex, Black identities are also complex and multidimensional. Some individuals define their group membership by racial identity (i.e., society sees me as Black, therefore I am) and/or by sharing a linked fate (see McClain et al (2009). Further, multi-dimensionality of Black identity can be seen in the following diagram (see McClain et al 2009):

National/Regional Origin →	Pan-ethnic Group Identity →	Shared Racial Minority Status
(Caribbean) →	(Jamaican) →	(Black)

From 1920s and 1960s, the history of the bond of Black group consciousness among native- and foreign-born Blacks is one that politicized Black racial identity, in which collective action was viewed as the best means for the group to improve its status and realize its shared interests.   Individuals' opinions and perspectives took a back seat to considerations that will benefit the Black race as a whole (Dawson 1994; Mangum 2008).   In many regards, group consciousness proved successful; many African Americans and those of Caribbean descent forged political alliances because of their unified interest for racial equality.   An important consideration for both native- and foreign born Blacks was the desire for social justice that served as a means for overcoming racial discrimination. Hence, they collaborated and focused their political interests on a New York City-wide level.   For example, in the 1930s, once Blacks were finally allowed to join community associations and clubs, their political presence was immediately felt. Through the early 1950s and 1960s people such as Shirley Chisholm, Bertram Baker, George Fleary, all of Caribbean heritage, wielded political influence in many major American cities including Brooklyn's communities (Moore, 1984).

By the mid-1960s, however, collaborative political interests and activity of African Americans and Caribbean immigrants underwent significant changes.   Moore (1984) attributes this change to political strides made by the Civil Rights movement.   Others such as Basch (1992:158-159) suggest that massive post-1965 Caribbean immigration coupled with the post-Civil Rights Movements' effect on softening of American racial barriers and attitudes resulted in Caribbeans emphasizing that they were an ethnically distinct group as well as a race.   Scholars (Bryce-Laporte 1972; Waters 1999) argue that post-1965 Caribbean immigrants emphasize their ethnic and cultural distinctiveness as a way to avoid the increasing racial stigmatization associated with native-born Blacks when they first arrive to the United States.

In many ways, the increase in racial-ethnic immigrant diversity transformed the Black American narrative--Black group consciousness-- and, consequently the opinions Black ethnics have toward each other as well as themselves. By asserting an ethnic identity, recent Caribbean immigrants attempt to override racial group identification, thus giving rise to a distinct set of interests or attitudes different from African Americans. One stereotype of Caribbeans is that they see themselves as hard-working, ambitious, conscious about being a Black person but not overly-sensitive or obsessed with race, and committed to education and family (Waters 1999). This stereotype also suggests that Caribbeans see African Americans as lazy, disorganized and having a lax attitude toward family life and child-raising (Vickerman 1999). It can be argued that Caribbean immigrants' assertion of a Caribbean ethnic identity or distinctiveness is used as a device to stress their distance from African Americans and to cultural values that they perceive are more consistent with American middle-class values. On the other hand, one stereotype of African Americans is that they view Caribbean immigrants as selfish, exploited in the workplace, and oblivious to racial tensions and politics in the United States (see Kasinitz 1992; Waters 1994). Because of these stereotypes, the basis of collaboration between Caribbean immigrants and African Americans, which was a stronghold for several decades, became limited.

This shift in group identity and consciousness has meant an increase in the perception, held by a few long-time residents of Central Brooklyn, that there are more competitors threatening fewer resources from being distributed equally in the Black community. In addition to the existence of Black-ethnic competition, some African American community members shared that there are African Americans who are frustrated with recent Caribbean immigrants who do not acknowledge that anti-Blackness continues today nor see the eminent need to rally together around the cause of their oppression (the blackness of their skin) and operate as a group in order to rid themselves of the low social status assigned to them (see also Bassey 2007; Biko 1971;Tarca 2005).

When asked to compare the experiences of recent Caribbean immigrants to African Americans, these African American community members suggested African Americans are more likely to have higher levels of racial group consciousness than Caribbean immigrants. These participants contend that because of African Americans' experience with centuries-worth of prejudice and discrimination, recent Caribbean immigrants enter the United States are somewhat unfamiliar with the history and instances of coalition building between African Americans and their Caribbean immigrant predecessors. Many participants go on to suggest that it is Caribbean immigrants' pre-migrant knowledge that informs them that while they may enter as part of a stigmatized minority group, they will not face the same impermeable color line as long as there is an emphasis on diversity of language and culture unless they share a stereotype of a Black phenotype typically associated with African Americans. Hence, the African American perception of the consequences of Caribbean ethnic distinctiveness and the assertion Caribbean ethnicity amongst Caribbean immigrants contributes to the split between these two groups in the central Brooklyn community.

The interesting fact that must be addressed here is the assumption that because African Americans' and Caribbean immigrants' share similar phenotypes both groups should share a degree of loyalty and political perspective. This assumption is based on the belief that a shared Black racial identity (or African ancestry) is sufficient to ensure a strong bond of political affinity for even the most recent Caribbean immigrant. It incorrectly implies that social bonds are based on biology and race. In fact, according to social science discourse, the category of race is not natural, consistent, or stable; racial identities do not exist apart from, or are unaffected by the social environment, particularly for those immigrants who have recently arrived. Racial categories are not fully predictive of ethnic unity. The mere fact that each group experiences varying levels and forms of discrimination and anti-Blackness (overt and covert) does not provide grounds for a connection on the basis of race alone. Caribbean immigrants and African Americans have different experiences with discrimination with regard to American racism and each other, thus a shared standpoint is difficult to forge on how to best advance their own and other Black ethnics' interests. For The Caribbean Service Center, the inter-group split between African Americans and Caribbean immigrants also creates a dilemma for the ethnic-identified and movement organization because this tension hinders its ability to mobilize the community to gain resources and support to support Blacks in the central Brooklyn area (see Rogers 2004, 2006; Su 2009).

Politics of Mobilizing Racial-Ethnic, Immigrant Communities

Many scholars and community leaders suggest that participating in local politics is the best option for racial-ethnic groups, including immigrants seeking inclusion into American society and gaining access to social services (Erie 1988; Gilliam and Kaufman 1998; Gurin, Hatchett, and Jackson 1989; Myrdal 1944; Tate 1991; West 1993). The importance of Black, immigrant political incorporation is related to the notion of empowerment--both symbolic and actual. Gilliam and Kaufman (1998:742) assert that for Blacks in particular, political empowerment means that as "Blacks become more politically engaged, they are visibly incorporated into local political structures," and therefore are more likely to be able to ensure policy responsiveness to their concerns.

When working with disenfranchised and marginalized racial-ethnic, immigrant communities, community-based organizations and their staff need political power and influence to acquire the resources needed to help clients (see Dunst, Trivette, and Deal, 1988; Hodges, Burwell, and Ortega 1998; Parsons 1991; Reissman 1990; Solomon 1987). As simple as it seems to identify what needs to be done, The Caribbean Service Center faces significant challenges. Its leaders and staff understand that in exchange for local politicians' attention to Black, immigrant communities, they must urge their Caribbean immigrant clients to become U.S. citizens and encourage Black community members to contribute to the political system via voting. The Caribbean Service Center recognized that establishing Caribbean immigrant and African American communities as a political power base (i.e., having the ability to vote politicians into office), is extremely important to its own credibility and success. Indeed, a community-based organization's ability or inability to mobilize members of a community to support a political candidate, for example, will determine how much attention politicians focus on the community.

Despite The Caribbean Service Center's efforts to urge its clients and community members to vote, the community's lack of involvement in local politics means that state and federal policies do not address the issues of native and foreign-born Blacks. In other words, politicians respond best to constituents who vote. Because many politicians' political success depends on the happiness of their constituents, politicians work hard to address their constituents' needs. When a collective does not vote, they fail to command the attention of politicians. The majority of The Caribbean Service Center's staff, founders, and leaders feel that the Caribbean immigrant and African American community's lack of involvement in local politics will lead to the continuation of the social problems that persist in the central Brooklyn Black community.

When asked whether there was a significant difference between Caribbean/African American communities and other ethnic groups with regard to their level of political participation, many responded "absolutely yes." Board member Marshall Jones suggests that,

Whether [African American] or West Indian [Caribbean], we want to feel that our plight is one that is validated--accepted. Oftentimes, community members feel that other groups are treated better than we are; that they are given certain exceptions and it's unfair. Many Blacks want to feel politicians and elected officials actually care about the situations that affect us most. With that, we then feel confident in their abilities to represent us. Unfortunately, this level of confidence in local officials does not exist; particularly when Blacks see local officials and the police protect other ethnic groups and not us; what happens [is that] Black Americans and the immigrants become disenchanted.

Participants cited one ethnic group in particular, Jews, as a population that Blacks, both native- and foreign-born, compete with for attention and protection of New York City officials. Occurrences, such as the "Crown Heights Riot" in August 1991, add to the perception that Jews, including Hasidic Jews in the area, have certain rights, privileges, and the protection of local officials that are not extended to Blacks both native and foreign-born because Jews are white. The disenchantment that Marshall Jones referred to, at best, articulates the persistent frustration many Blacks in central Brooklyn feel about the fact that other non-Black ethnics' rights and needs are better protected and validated than theirs. Blacks view the Jewish community as a powerful ethnic group that maintains an economic stronghold in New York City's political and social negotiation process because of their whiteness (Brodkin 1998; Greenberg 1997; Rieder 1995). Specifically, scholars Greenberg (1997) and Rieder (1995) who focus on Black and

Jewish relationships suggest that Blacks harbor, arguably, anti-Semitic views concerning Jews because of their perception of the Jewish community as powerful.

By "becoming white" (see Brodkin, 1998), Jews have been successful in appealing to politicians in ways Blacks have struggled to do. Scholars believe that Jews shifted from emphasizing an ethnic identity to identifying as a white racial group over time because, "most rewards and opportunities in America were apportioned not by ethnicity or religion but by race, and because most Jews were seen as white, Jews were no exception to this pattern" (Greenberg, 1997: 155). Because of their skin color, Jews were more successful in meeting with other white ethnic political leaders, collectively mobilizing the community and voting, and raising money in support of community concerns or political candidates, at rates much higher than Blacks and other racial-ethnics groups had in the past.

The Caribbean Service Center's leaders contend that Caribbean immigrants and African Americans are not unified and are not in agreement about the specific issues that affect both groups. They suggest the lack of unity or discord hinders mobilization and contributes to the apathy, community disintegration, transnationalism, and political cynicism that impede this community's political incorporation.

Implications of Ethnic Tension on Community Relations

Ethnic differentiation creates serious problems within central Brooklyn's Black and immigrant community. For African Americans, Caribbean distinctiveness is perceived as increasing contention and competition, thus making it difficult for the two groups to work together. Ethnic tensions, in effect, reduce the likelihood that Caribbean immigrants and African Americans will share a racial group identity that would in turn inform their social and political attitudes and behaviors. In fact, ethnic tensions make it difficult for the community to develop a strong power base from which its native- and foreign-born Black members can operate. Thus, the disharmony and antagonism that persist between these two groups accentuates competitiveness rather than cooperation, facilitating increased community disintegration and apathy.

Community disintegration and apathy--rooted in American racism--is the social climate that forces both Caribbean immigrants and African Americans to be prejudiced towards one another. Riesman and Glazer (1950) state that a community in which apathy prevails is likely a community with already low levels of integration and one in which attitudes and practices create resistance to developing active cooperation of all members. As it stands in central Brooklyn, there is not a strong, integrated or unified community feeling that supports and integrates all members into one functioning unit. This lack of integration leads to Caribbean immigrants' and African Americans' apathy.

The community's apathy is fueled by the stereotype that Caribbean immigrants are not committed to the social and political issues that affect people of African ancestry in America because Caribbean immigrants are connected to their homelands. Some of The Caribbean Service Center's staff and leaders referred to community members' impressions of this prominent political and social separateness as being related to recent immigrants' focus on their homelands and the overall political cynicism African Americans and Caribbean immigrants have about the American social and political system. Rasheeda Hines, a prominent Brooklyn civil servant and community leader explains,

> Caribbean people, today, are very much concerned with what's going on back home. These immigrants are very different from the ones that came here generations ago. The mindset is: come to America, get an education, make some money, send barrels home, help who you can help to come up so that they can do the same, and leave. The immigrants from years ago may have sent things back home and were concerned with the issues of their people back home, but the immediate intention was to make their stay in America the best they can. I think that's why the older generations were more politically active than the ones are today. Our communities are so split it is difficult for us all to come to the table because we think no one understands the other or that certain issues are more important.

Many of the community leaders interviewed suggest that transnationalism contributes to the community's apathy. In this regard, sustained attention to their home countries gives Caribbean ethnicity a transnational focus (see Rogers 2001). Transnationalism, as explored by scholars Glick-Schiller, Basch, and Szanton-Blanc (1992), Portes, et al (1999), Levitt (2001), and Waldinger (2004), focuses on migration connections between home and host societies. Transnationalism is more than the dual connections immigrants make between their home and receiving societies. Immigrants maintain a connection to their home society that is more than simply caring for family left behind through telephone calls, letters, and remittances. They also maintain symbolic loyalties. Of the few The Caribbean Service Center's clients I spoke to informally, many described the ways they participate in the economic and political life of their home country--all with the intention of returning one day. Some send equipment and supplies to churches and schools. Some donate money to their native countries through The Caribbean Service Center and other community-based organizations for disaster relief projects. These Caribbean immigrants are also an important resource for their home society's industrial development because they send remittances and other resources that contribute to the islands' development.

These ties to their home countries however, make it less likely for these immigrants to establish similar connections to their new societies. Wanda Martines, program manager in Legal Services noted that immigrants' intention to return to their homelands seems extreme to outsiders. She suggests that some clients will display such a strong loyalty to their home country by supporting their home society even if it means that they can risk losing all they have attained in the United States (i.e., a house, car, prestigious job). Wanda adds,

> We have clients who may not understand the nuances of their visas, come in with questions about their rights while here in the States. These clients are interesting to me because they come here for school, mostly, and are educated, will meet a person, date them, and instead of applying for residency to stay and start a new life and family they let their visas expire because they don't want to give up on [their home country]. Some of them want to return to places like Haiti where people are being murdered and there's a lot of civil unrest just so they

don't have to give up citizenship or any rights to home. I mean, it can be crazy to understand, and I don't get it sometimes but this attitude is common.

Many immigrants believe that acquiring full membership within American society (i.e., citizenship) will force them to lose rights and privileges in their home countries. A common rationale is that national identities are mono-national. From this perspective, to acquire a new national identity, by necessity, entails giving up an existing national identity. The unwillingness to vote or seek full membership is related to the idea that many Caribbean immigrants feel that one day, they will return to their home countries. Hence, immigrants' connections to their homelands contribute to the African American view that Caribbean people are apathetic to the social conditions of Blacks in the States. As Hendricks (1974) and Papademtriou (1983) have argued, the problem with the lack of Caribbean's political participation in today's New York City's polities is a result of their continued support of their home societies and their misunderstanding of the American citizenship process. As Board member Maria Hernandez suggests,

> Many people within the community are misinformed or have a lack of information regarding what the actual issues are in Brooklyn and how they can properly inform themselves to vote. Some even think that if they become citizens, they give up their rights to their country. That's simply not true. In fact, many islands allow for dual citizenships. Knowing this, for me, that's how I came to become a citizen also. For West Indians in New York, I guess they don't necessarily see themselves being vested here because they came here temporarily, they're planning to leave any way to go back home. Some are still distracted by the issues that their families left behind face, which I don't blame them. But, what about here? They live here! They work here! Raise children and grandchildren here! Sometimes, I think that this pride and lack of knowledge makes us kind of ignorant about not participating politically.

Immigrants' apathy toward the American political process is also related to the experiences and perceptions immigrants bring with them and the context of their arrival. Portes and Rumbaut (1996: 107) suggest that "immigrants differed in their past political socialization, commitment to return, and national situations left behind. The combination of these factors affects not only their stance in American politics but also their orientations and behavior towards their homeland." Prior to their immigration, recent Caribbean immigrants hold ideals and beliefs regarding American politics which stem from their interaction with their home country's politics as well as their perception of the United States' handling of its domestic affairs.

Many of The Caribbean Service Center's Caribbean clients left countries whose government and politics tend to be highly corrupt and its citizens depend on bribery for protection. Upon arrival, these immigrants believe, and often have experiences, that perpetuate the belief that the American government is corrupt and unjust in its treatment of racial-ethnics. Accustomed to navigating through politics by their own informal networks or class status, Caribbean immigrants are skeptical of participating in American politics. The overt racialism that exists in America perpetuates Caribbean immigrants' willingness to stay loyal to their home country's corrupt government because they feel that they can make a difference and still benefit from their home island if they continue their investment in the island's politics. Hence, Caribbean immigrants' transnational attachments factors heavily in their political thinking, and help to explain why their choice to focus on ethnicity as a primary mode of group identification does not mirror that of African Americans (Rogers 2001).

In addition to transnationalism, political cynicism is a factor that contributes to the inability of today's central Brooklyn's Caribbean immigrant and African American community members to unite and mobilize for the equitable distribution of resources and better provisions of services. Many members of the African American and Caribbean American community live in modest neighborhoods, pay taxes, join unions, and may be members of churches. Their voices, however, are seldom heard when it comes to issues of urban life. Often, political voice is measured by voter turnout. Blacks (both native and foreign-born), ages 18 to 30 years, in the United States have lower rates of voter turnout than any other ethnic group. While African Americans and Caribbean Americans, like early 20th century white ethnics (i.e., the Irish-Americans), understand that voting means having political control, their relationship to the political process is historically and racially different. It has stunted their political participation over time.

Caribbean Immigrant and African American Sentiments toward Political Participation

The political process for white ethnics at the turn of the twentieth century is seen as dramatically different from today's racial-ethnic immigrant groups. The early Irish, for example, were successful in taking over City Hall with political control and were able to build an economic base as a result. Irish political power was built with trust and loyalties to political parties, organized block voting, and mobilization of community members with memories of oppression (see Sleeper 1990; Traub 1994). With all of these factors, the Irish were able to gain political power and trust in the political system. In contrast, African Americans' low level of political participation is due in large part to their distrust of the electoral process. According to Derrick Bell (2004) minimal Black political participation levels can be dated as far back as 1832 when Alexis de Tocqueville wrote about the dismal rates in which free African Americans exercised their civil rights. Tocqueville stated that "the truth is that [African Americans] are not disinclined to vote, but they are afraid of being maltreated; in this country the law is sometimes unable to maintain its authority without the support of the majority. But in this case, the majority entertains very strong prejudices against Blacks, and the magistrates are unable to protect them in the exercise of the legal rights [of voting]" (1969:344). Until the establishment of the Voting Rights Act of 1965, government sanctioned groups and the Klu Klux Klan used violence and other forms of intimidation as well as policies that prevented African Americans from voting.

Although many states in the north, like New York, abolished such policies during the late 1920s, the distrust that developed as a consequence was based on African Americans' experiences with the government's inability to protect them and take their claims seriously. This distrust is still persistent today amongst both African Americans and Caribbean people. African Americans are frustrated and disillusioned with the political system, thus, decreasing the likelihood for them to have confidence and a strong desire to participate in the political process. For Caribbean immigrants, the lack of social policy or adequate representation for all those that share an African ancestry in the judicial system contributes to their perception that the American government does not provide them or African Americans with equal treatment. The historical racial barriers that block African Americans from mainstream politics, as a result, contribute to Caribbean immigrants' maintenance of their transnational ties and their assertion of an ethnic and immigrant identity over a Black racial identity.

Caribbean immigrants' maintenance of transnational ties and hesitancy to participate in the American political system contributes to African Americans' frustration with Caribbeans, thus, leading to the persistence of ethnic tensions. Rogers (2001, 2004) suggests that African Americans' sense of racial group attachment or consciousness--i.e., a Black racial identity--overrides ethnic identities (e.g., Caribbean, South African) because of their belief that race shapes life chances and to a large degree determines what happens to all those that share in an African ancestry. Since African Americans' political thinking is not bound to their own ethnic group's interests but instead bound to their racial group's interests, there is often a sense of betrayal African Americans have toward recent Caribbean immigrants and some Caribbean Americans for not "joining the cause."

Serving Two Masters: How The Caribbean Service Center Shapes Inter-group Dynamics

Caribbean immigrants come to identify with African Americans on issues of discrimination and inequality the longer they stay in the United States. Yet, recently arrived Caribbean immigrants still distance themselves from African Americans to avoid downward mobility. In communities like central Brooklyn where recently arrived Caribbean immigrants live in urban, working class neighborhoods with other Blacks, it is found that Caribbean immigrants are more likely to assert an ethnic-identified identity as a way to distance themselves from African Americans. As stated by The Caribbean Service Center's Board and Director Dr. Gary Whits, the increased likelihood for Caribbean immigrants who live in neighborhoods with more Blacks to express an ethnic identity, point to a common explanation of competition and animosity. According to Rogers (2004), competition between Caribbean immigrants and African Americans for scarce resources may push these two groups further apart rather than closer together.

Recognizing the role residential segregation plays in forcing Caribbeans and African Americans to live in close proximity to one another, ethnic-identified organizations are critical to reducing tensions and coalition building (Su 2009). In the case of central Brooklyn, The Caribbean Service Center's support and encouragement of their Caribbean immigrant clients' ethnicity and culture, contributes to Caribbeans' social distancing and pro-Caribbean sentiments. The organization's promotion of Caribbean culture and identity is, in many ways, geared toward providing newly arrived Caribbean immigrants an environment that relies on beliefs and values that are cherished by many Caribbean people. At the same time, The Caribbean Service Center's Board and Director also had to strategize ways to reduce the tension between Caribbeans and African Americans. What is most striking about The Caribbean Service Center's efforts to reduce these tensions is that it required the organization to expand its client and staff base to include African Americans and other non-Caribbean groups. According to Aldrich (1999), an organization's ability to survive a changing environment is to evolve. The Caribbean Service Center was faced with the dilemma of adapting to demographic changes while assisting in the adaptation and acculturation of their Caribbean clients into American culture. The Caribbean Service Center had to adapt and forge alliances with other immigrant and African American groups to avoid undercutting their efforts to secure sociopolitical approval.

Like other community-based organizations that rely heavily on public support from the community and external funding agencies, The Caribbean Service Center could not afford to lose support from African American community leaders and supporters. The Caribbean Service Center's founders and Board knew they had to convince its staff that their venture to expand its client population was appropriate and right given the existing need for equitable distribution of resources and better provisions of services for all Blacks in the community. Even still, The Caribbean Service Center's most fervent African American critics contend that organization has not been successful in its efforts to integrate African Americans into its client base. In this regard, The Caribbean Service Center's focus on the Caribbean community has, indirectly, contributed to polarizing the social issues of Caribbean immigrants and African Americans and made it harder for the organization and its community leaders to advocate effectively on behalf of central Brooklyn's Black ethnic and immigrant community. By facilitating social distancing and ethnic distinctiveness, The Caribbean Service Center indirectly confirms the dominant group's perception that racial ideologies toward African Americans are true. Take for instance 1960s organizations such as The Black Panther Party (BPP), The Rainbow Coalition, or the Student Nonviolent Coordinating Committee (SNCC). Similar to The Caribbean Service Center, The Black Panther Party (BPP), The Rainbow Coalition, and the Student Nonviolent Coordinating Committee (SNCC) developed and instituted a variety of social programs designed to reduce poverty and improve the access to and utilization of health care and social services among racial-ethnic communities. These organizations also recognized that different racial-ethnic communities who share histories of being oppressed should organize around their own set of issues. Yet, different from today's immigrant and ethnic identified organizations, many of the 1960s African American identified organizations mentioned above had organizational goals that focused on urban activism and Black politics.

In contrast, The Caribbean Service Center's organizational goals, even with its political implications, emphasize culture. Because the emphasis is on culture as opposed to promoting a political agenda, racial-ethnic immigrant identified organizations are perceived by the dominant group as less confrontational, more inclusive, and thus, safe. The impetus for The Caribbean Service Center's promotion of a Caribbean ethnicity is, arguably, the subconscious belief that the dominant group will view Caribbean immigrants as "different Blacks" with "special" needs and treat them more positively. Unfortunately, by assisting these new immigrants' ability to carve out an ethnic niche, The Caribbean Service Center inadvertently impedes community integration thus, making overcoming ethnic tensions difficult.

As a community-based organization also responsible for responding to and reducing the increasing social problems that persist in the community, The Caribbean Service Center's Board, staff, and community leaders recognized that the inter-group tensions that exist hinder the organization's efforts and strategies to effectively and efficiently serve the community. Some of The Caribbean Service Center's Board members have suggested that the organization develop programs and activities that focus on issues affecting both Caribbean immigrants in Brooklyn and in their immigrant home societies as well as including the interests and concerns of African American community members. Archibald Dubnet, Board member, explains,

> The key is to make the entire community feel comfortable about us as an organization. It is good business practice to be inclusive, yes, but for the purpose of the work we do as an organization for the community, West Indians--Caribbean people and African Americans, we must make it so that everyone's voice is heard. It is truly about empowering people and perspectives. So, we adapt, change, evolve, and collaborate, and embrace diverse perspectives. That means offering broader programming, forums, and so on.

Yet, incorporating African American interests into the organization's activities creates a dilemma for The Caribbean Service Center. While leaders of The Caribbean Service Center want to reduce ethnic tensions and mobilize Caribbean immigrants and African Americans in central Brooklyn, many community members would become confused as to the aims and specific direction of the organization's efforts (whether efforts were based on Caribbean nationality or Black racial consciousness). Because The Caribbean Service Center originated from the grassroots activity of Caribbean nurses in central Brooklyn, whose organizing and activities was aimed at increasing health resources for Caribbean immigrants, the organization's current efforts to integrate native-born Blacks would seem contradictory to both African Americans and Caribbean immigrants. Some of The Caribbean Service Center's community members expressed concern as to whether it was possible to unify the interest of the community when members have different histories, issues, or concerns (e.g., immigration and civil rights). As Clement Thomas, a community leader suggests, the ethnic tensions that persist between African Americans and recent Caribbean immigrants is,

> ...nonsense quite frankly because at the end of the struggle, it shouldn't matter whether you can trace your roots from the Caribbean or from Durham in North Carolina, you don't have to have a Caribbean accent to feel some of the constraints that

the immigrant has and vice versa. The focus should be on getting people to vote and having diverse political representation. Now if you want to have your agenda recognized, you have to have the people there to articulate your agenda and you must have people in Albany, NY and you must have people in City Hall. I think that is part of the dilemma that we face. Divide and Conquer. Yes, we have issues that spring from our immigrant status and the same goes for American Blacks and their status here, but we all have to be able to fight the right battle that addresses us, as Black people together if we are to progress as a people.

The difficulty The Caribbean Service Center faces in integrating Caribbean ethnicity and Black racial consciousness is that its leaders assume that both Caribbean immigrants and African Americans will develop and share similar responses to the challenges racism pose in their lives. While it is true that both groups' experience with racism has an effect on their mobility, each group has different reactions to American racism--e.g., recent Caribbean immigrants' transnational attachments. Unfortunately for this central Brooklyn community, the promise of Black unity between Caribbean immigrants and African Americans will diminish as long as racial stratification and discrimination exists in America.

The challenges to reducing inter-group conflict between African American and Caribbean immigrant are eminent and the potential benefits of greater collaboration and unity between these groups are also significant. Increasing collaboration and a unifying agenda that attempts to best advance Caribbean immigrant and African American ethnic interests will require the joint effort of both ethnic populations and the organizations that serve them. In many ways, ethnic-identified organizations' efforts have implications for coalition-building efforts.

By virtue of its role as a community-based organization, The Caribbean Service Center can shape inter-group dynamics. The Caribbean Service Center must navigate through community politics in order to meet its community's needs and address their political interests while sharing knowledge and resources among community members. Reducing ethnic tensions would require establishing a cooperative Black agenda and providing community programming that will empower Caribbeans and African Americans and lead them to politically mobilize and demand more resources. For organizations to advocate on the behalf of and support the integration of its community members, there must to be a focus on the need to share common ideals of viability and survival despite their heterogeneous ethnic and national elements.

The Caribbean Service Center, community members, and other organizations must set priorities for uniting the community in the form of policy advocacy around key issues. Yet, these issues must be perceived as non-controversial, such as health care, in order for the entire community to unite and sustain its cooperative work (Kirwan Institute 2009). To successfully do this, the community must be engaged in a way that members view themselves as not only beneficiaries but shapers of community collaboration with other Black ethnics, in spite of their transnational connections to the Caribbean or negative perceptions of American political system.

This is very difficult work. Yet, the possibilities for The Caribbean Service Center to continue to advocate for better social and health services for their diverse racial-ethnic and Caribbean immigrant constituents are endless. There are, however, several questions that remain. Considering the internal impediments of unifying this diverse Black community, will The Caribbean Service Center maintain its reputation in the community as a Caribbean organization or will it adopt a more Black organizational identity as a way to promote a unified Black agenda and gain the support of African Americans in the community? And, at what cost would this mean to the incorporation and assimilation of Caribbean immigrants, including those who identify specifically as Latino? Also, considering the role of racism, if organizations like The Caribbean Service Center are successful in unifying and politically mobilizing their Caribbean and African American communities, will the government and local officials successfully respond to their demands the same way the government met the demands of white ethnics? Only time will tell.

CHAPTER 6

Final Word

In this case study on Black Caribbean ethnic identity, I have sought to develop a sense of the process by which organizations influence the assimilation, immigrant corporation, and identity construction of recent Caribbean immigrants in central Brooklyn. I have argued that community-based organizations, and particularly ethnic identified organizations such as The Caribbean Service Center, play a significant role in influencing their immigrant clients' maintenance of a Caribbean ethnic identity. Also, I have argued that the existence of a Caribbean-identified organization, located in a densely populated native- and foreign-born Black enclave, can impact its Caribbean immigrant clients' segmented assimilation paths and their rates of assimilation. Through its organizational culture, climate, programming, and services, the organization's promotion and celebration of Caribbean ethnicity slows the rate of traditional immigrant incorporation (i.e., contact, competition, accommodation, and assimilation) because many immigrants *choose* to hold on to island traditions and maintain Caribbean identity consciousness. At the same time, I also suggested that Caribbean immigrants' participation in ethnic-identified organizations speeds up the rate by which they internalize the norms and values of American society including their understanding of race and identity, and the facilitation and utilization of Black Caribbean ethnic identity options.

At the crux of my argument, I have pushed for fresh thinking on the concept of race and Black identity by focusing on a community-based organization, its history, practices, and the internal and external polities, and the ways it influences its clients understanding of ethnic identity. Today's scholarship on recent immigrant identity has moved the analysis of race, ethnic identity construction, assimilation, and community toward greater complexity. But these insights have not extended to research on the specific role community-based organizations play in influencing assertions of identity.

Also, in this study I explored some of the community issues that arise as a result of Caribbean immigrants' maintenance of an ethnic identity--i.e., tensions between Caribbeans and African Americans--and The Caribbean Service Center's indirect role in perpetuating such tensions. I suggested that through its services, The Caribbean Service Center not only encourages its Caribbean immigrants to selectively assimilate (carve out an ethnic niche) within mainstream society but also creates a tendency for its Caribbean clients to internalize and, consequently reject African American stereotypes through social distancing (Vickerman 1999). As a result, this tendency reinforces differences between Caribbeans and African Americans and allowed for the perpetuation of racial stigmatization and inequality to persist in central Brooklyn.

Cost and Benefits of Organizations on Black Caribbean Ethnic Identity

The Caribbean Service Center has been vital to the survival of racial-ethnic immigrants in central Brooklyn over the last few decades. Those who reside in the area and participate in its community-based activities and efforts perceive The Caribbean Service Center as an important part of the Caribbean immigrant community. The Caribbean Service Center works closely with members of that community and focuses its efforts on empowering Caribbean people through delivery of individual and family services. These efforts are intended to help acculturate their newly arrived clients to a highly political and socially complex American racial system. The Caribbean Service Center developed programming initiatives primarily designed to provide ethnically relevant and culturally-sensitive services and politically mobilize and organize Caribbean people in the community. In addition, its Caribbean staff members consciously help their clients critique oppressive social arrangements by providing them with ethnic-identified strategies to negotiate a social service system that historically discriminates against Black ethnics and immigrants.

The Caribbean Service Center's staff assistance and staff encouragement of client ethnic strategies is an important ingredient of ethnic empowerment. Because staff members share similar ethnic and immigrant experiences as their Caribbean clients, staff members help to raise client awareness of their own circumstances, strengths, resources, and ethnic option choices. Through The Caribbean Service Center's staff-client interaction, there is a parallel process of ethnic empowerment for both staff workers and clients. This process is facilitated by two main factors: 1) the organization (i.e., its history, culture and climate, and structure); and 2) ethnic connection to Caribbean-ness.

The Caribbean Service Center recognized that creating an empowering organizational culture was an important strategy for connecting to the Caribbean community. An essential feature of its organizational culture is the willingness and capacity of its Caribbean founders, Board, and staff members to respond to federal and state policies regulating social service and health programs, and tailor services to these particular circumstances. Staff members respond to their clients' needs by serving as their advocates and mentors, and professionals. Clients and staff members alike are empowered--are able to share, discuss, and identify societal conditions that foster powerlessness. Through its organizational culture, ideology, practices and informal techniques of providing efficacy-enhancing information, The Caribbean Service Center creates an opportunity for Caribbean immigrants to assert a Caribbean identity within the United States.

In contrast to other community-based organizations where Black ethnic identities are not celebrated but American assimilation is promoted, The Caribbean Service Center's Caribbean immigrant clients learn from staff members that ethnicity does matter (e.g., to caseworkers and policy makers) and of the importance of developing ethnic strategies that will assist them in obtaining better services for themselves and their families. The Caribbean Service Center's staff is able to demonstrate its commitment to the community and to its clients. This demonstration increases client compliance and organizational support. In effect, ethnic empowerment is a long-term process that both influences and is transformed by an organization's own evolution and commitment to the community it serves (Gutierrez et al 1995; Kieffer 1984). Hence, The Caribbean Service Center's commitment to the Caribbean community, via ethnic empowerment, increases its ability to influence their racial-ethnic, immigrant clients' understanding of race and ethnic identity.

Community-based and ethnic-identified organizations, like The Caribbean Service Center, expose racial-ethnic immigrants to the realities of racism and discrimination that are related to African American stereotypes. In turn, realities of racism and discrimination leave racial-ethnic immigrants to face the choice of acquiescing to these stereotypes, establishing a distinct Caribbean identity, or alternating between these identities in order to improve their life chances. Therefore, The Caribbean Service Center's staff, clients, and community members are more likely to choose to celebrate a variety of Caribbean identity options as a strategy to avoid racial stigmatization typically associated with African Americans.

Choosing to celebrate and assert distinct ethnic identities within various contexts, is in large part, based on the understanding that the mainstream society's conception of the ethnic group will govern the group's long term life chances and opportunities through federal, state, and local policies. As discussed in Chapter Three, the dominant society's treatment of Blacks and Caribbean people shaped the demographics of the central Brooklyn community, the identification of problems, and the availability of resources for those needing services. The Caribbean Service Center became the organization that, in effect, reflected the culture and society in which the organization is lodged. In other words, The Caribbean Service Center's ideology, mission, goals, and agenda--to support Caribbean and racial-ethnic, immigrant communities--was a response to the government's unwillingness to adequately serve Caribbeans and other racial-ethnics of central Brooklyn.

While being a Caribbean-identified organization can be perceived as positive in this central Brooklyn community, it can also be argued that The Caribbean Service Center indirectly focuses attention to racial and ethnic differences between Black ethnic groups. The wave of Caribbean immigration in the mid-twentieth century established a set of tensions between Caribbeans and African Americans that persist to this day. Although these two Black ethnic populations share a common history of slavery/colonialism, racial segregation, and economic struggle, the notion of "what it means to be Black" is more than being defined as "not White." The question of what it means to be Black is always a complicated one, and neither the end of segregation nor the emergence of a Black middle-class has done much to lessen the complexity (see Rogers 2001).

America's struggle with issues of race and ethnicity--particularly its stereotypical characterizations of African Americans--has served to exacerbate and fuel ethnic tensions between native- and foreign-born Blacks. In fact, America's own definitions of and relationship with African Americans draw attention to the stereotype that Black immigrants (i.e., Caribbean Blacks) are the "better Blacks." The larger society's conceptions of these ethnic differences also plague organizations' and clients' views about the treatment of African Americans and Caribbeans in the community. Ethnic-identified organizations like The Caribbean Service Center internalize these racial ideologies within its organizational culture and implement policies that affect the formation and the maintenance of Black ethnic identities of their clients. One of the ways Caribbean clients learn the social meaning behind asserting particular Black identities is within this organizational environment.

Constructing and negotiating Black ethnic identities is a dialectical process which involves Caribbean immigrants' opinions of their own ethnic group and the opinions and treatment of their ethnic group by others. Caribbeans learn early on, in their interaction with African Americans and other racial and ethnic groups in the community, a popular Zora Neale Hurston maxim, "all of your skin-folk are not your kinfolk" (1942/2006). Despite island-specific differences, linguistic differences, religious differences, class differences, skin-tone differences (i.e., lighter or darker hued), and other diversities within the Caribbean population, many recent Caribbean immigrants adopt paths of selective assimilation (see Portes and Zhou 1993), acknowledging that "not everyone who is your color is your kind." To be able to access better resources Caribbeans may create this strategy. The Caribbean Service Center's community members also point to institutional circumstances or conditions that influence the way Caribbean immigrants think about race.

As an organization, The Caribbean Service Center provides a space to choose to identify as Jamaican, Caribbean, or Black,—it creates the possibility for these categories to be more flexible and dynamic. Caribbeans' high comfort level to assert specific Caribbean ethnic identities within The Caribbean Service Center reinforces distinctive behavioral and cultural patterns different from African Americans.

Thus, increasing Caribbean immigrants' distinctive sense of ethnicity tightens ethnic boundaries and perpetuates ethnic tensions between themselves and African Americans despite The Caribbean Service Center's concern to create a more unified Black community.

The Future Role of Black, Ethnic Community-based Organizations

This analysis contributes to our understanding of the incorporation of Caribbean immigrants in the United States. Specifically, the research highlights the complex ways contact with other co-ethnic Caribbeans within community-based organizations shape Caribbean immigrants' ethnic identity assertions. In line with the segmented assimilation model of incorporation, the meanings Caribbean immigrants attach to their Caribbean identity are shaped not only by how they are treated within the United States but also by the skills and ideologies that they bring with them from the Caribbean (see Benson 2006).

Because many of The Caribbean Service Center's clients are newly arrived immigrants, they hold more fluid notions regarding their ethnic identities. According to segmented assimilation models, these clients' incorporation depends on how the Caribbean migrant group is received in the central Brooklyn community and in community-based organizations. Thus, community-based organizations like The Caribbean Service Center have the chief role in facilitating the process and variation in the way Caribbean immigrants develop and assert their ethnic identity.

Ethnically-identified community-based organizations like The Caribbean Service Center assist clients in navigating through bureaucracies, accessing and utilizing services they need the most, as well as helping clients find recognition and status in their new country, The United States. These organizations are responsible for implementing ethnic-based services to their clients while buffering clients from the harsh realities of American society. In the case of Black Caribbean immigrants, The Caribbean Service Center attempted to buffer its Caribbean immigrant clients by providing a place where ethnic diversity could be celebrated. Ethnic-identified organizations also have access to the community, visibility in the community, and intimate knowledge of the community's concerns and thereby seek to address the needs of the community it serves when government agencies fail to do so. Thus, as long as immigration of Caribbean,

Latino, African, and other racial and ethnic groups continues to increase, racial and ethnic immigrants will continue to rely on community-based organizations. Considering the role community-based organizations play in facilitating the ethnic identity construction and assertion of Caribbean immigrants, I contend that findings in this case study point to the complexities of Black ethnic identity development and American racism. This complexity must be situated within the context of persisting tensions between Black Caribbean immigrants and African Americans, the hierarchy of culturally related positive and negative images promoted by mainstream society about both native and foreign-born Blacks, and the internalization of these images and stereotypes by Blacks and the community organizations that serve them. In effect, the larger implication of this study, I believe, is the impact racism has on a Black ethnic immigrant's identity construction as part of racial minority group and the positive symbols of self-concept and identity community-based organizations provide to their newly arrived immigrant client.

I want to conclude with an observation concerning the future role of Black ethnic-identified community-based organizations like The Caribbean Service Center. Although the future is, of course, uncertain, I believe that there will be a continuing need for Black ethnic and immigrant organizations as long as Black immigrants suffer "multiple levels of invisibility" (Bryce-Laporte 1979: 218). Bryce-Laporte (1979:219) suggests that Caribbean immigrants'

...distinctive problems and unique proclivities are generally overlooked or sublimated vis-à-vis the large non-white native minorities of the country, and they tend to be viewed and treated with the same disregard and discrimination which native Blacks suffer as visible minorities. Paradoxically, [Caribbeans] will suffer multiple invisibility because of their commonly shared visibility with their native born peers.

Thus, I believe that Caribbean immigrants' efforts to become more visible will lead to their increased ethnic identification and competition with African Americans for better social services and improved social status. Caribbean immigrant community members will continue to use ethnicity and ethnic identity options as potential resources to assist them in increasing visibility. While utilizing ethnicity as a resource or a tool of empowerment can be helpful to recent racial-ethnic, immigrants, the broader social implication behind an ethnic-designated community-based organization's role in contributing to ethnic identity options development and maintenance suggests that racial-ethnic discrimination and racial stigmatization will continue to persist.

The policy implication of this lies in the way organizational contexts influences how new racial-ethnic immigrants, such as Caribbean immigrants, behave, act, and react to their settings. In doing so, we need more social research that focuses on the ethnic identification choices Black and other racial-ethnic immigrants make within organizational settings. I have argued that the efforts of community-based organizations are an essential element to helping racial-ethnics create an imagined community (see Anderson 1983) as a way of developing a sense of understanding and control over their social reality. The experience of The Caribbean Service Center's founders, Board and staff members tells us that there is a continuing significance of American racism creating tensions in the community between Black immigrants and African Americans. The cycle of tension between native and foreign-born Blacks, and social and political disengagement by both Caribbean immigrants and African Americans must be broken.

Breaking this cycle involves developing policies that examine how a unified and integrated community can help shape the economic, political, and social opportunities that would benefit African Americans and Black immigrants and their second- and third generation descendants. Instead of continuing to compare native-born Blacks to recent racial-ethnic immigrant groups, hopefully, policies that elucidate the dynamic interplay race and ethnicity have in shaping the lives of people of African ancestry could point to the ways in which community-based organizations can assist its community members' to overcome racial stigmatization.

Hence, as long as race, racial stigmatization, and discrimination remain an inescapable fact of life for people of color, I contend that Black Caribbean ethnic identity options will continue to characterize the experiences of later generation racial and ethnic immigrants arriving to the United States. Yet, with each succeeding generation of "brown" immigrants hailing from Asia, Africa, and the Hispanic Caribbean, Black Caribbean ethnic identity options will also diverge from those held by earlier arrivals. The potential of this divergence begs for the following questions to be asked: how will language or bilingualism impact ethnic identity assertions of Black Caribbean immigrants who may have skin tones that fall within a color gradient from light to dark skin but also choose to identify as Latino/ Hispanic? Will Caribbean ethnicity reemerge as a pan-ethnic Latino identity while Black Caribbean identity emerges as a form of neo-African Americanism? Are these two types of identity assertions different from one another? Will these assertions lead to different acculturation outcomes for immigrants and their families?

While further research is required to address these questions, indeed I postulate that bilingual Caribbean immigrants, particularly those that self-identify as Black Hispanics and/or Afro-Hispanics, will experience multilayered hybridity and ambiguity regarding their own self-defined heritage and relationship to perceived meanings of Blackness and Hispanic ethnicity. In other words, multilayered hybridity and ambiguity may cause Black Hispanics to live within a broader, more fluid racial and ethnic range but also have specific racialized experiences. Perhaps different from their Anglophone Caribbean immigrant counterparts, Black Hispanics who chose to affirm their Hispanic Caribbean ethnicity as opposed to asserting a Black racial identity may be categorized by mainstream society as non-Black or as an "ambiguous other," depending on the social, political, and economic context of the time.

As scholars and community practitioners seek to understand the continued impact of diversity, ethnic ambiguity, and multiculturalism in the communities they serve, they must remain mindful that ethnic labels are socially constructed, self-applied, and applied by others. Such labels are equally as powerful and determining to the human condition of immigrants arriving to America.

Description of Positions and Demographic Information, New York

The Caribbean Service Center's Board of Directors are responsible for leading and supervising the organization. The role of the Board is to influence the behaviors of staff members in the interest of achieving particular organizational goals. They do this through establishing the organization's aims, goals, and long-and short-term agendas. Many of the Board members are involved in fundraising and political networking as a means to maintain the organization's legitimacy and increase its opportunity to receive public support. Currently, many of the founders and organizers of the movement serve on The Caribbean Service Center's Board.

As a grassroots-driven organization, The Caribbean Service Center needs the continued support of the community and the Board and the Executive Director look to the support of Community Leaders. Community leaders help articulate the needs and grievances of the community to the organization as well as assist the organization in remaining client-driven and community-focused. Community leaders that work within The Caribbean Service Center have been local politicians in the community or City, outreach members of local churches or benevolent associations, and professors from local community colleges and universities. Many community leaders have gone on to serve on its Board.

The Executive Director has the primary responsibility of setting the culture and climate of the organization. He or she is supposed to embody and express the ideology and purpose of the organization so that staff members are clear as to what the organization stands for. The Executive Director has authority and discretion over hiring of staff, the everyday tasks and routines of the various programs and its managers, and conducting evaluations on quality and effectiveness of service. In addition, the Executive Director is responsible for creating and establishing rapports with community groups as well as being the spokesperson on particular issues. For The Caribbean Service Center's first fifteen years, Sharon Higgins served as its Executive Director before moving on to City-wide politics. Although she resigned as Executive Director, Sharon Higgins continues to serve the organization as a member of the Board of Directors. Dr. Gary Whits took her place as the current Executive Director. Dr. Gary Whits continues to work with Sharon Higgins, who is instrumental in keeping The Caribbean Service Center an organization focused on putting Caribbean social, health, and economic needs and concerns on the political forefront.

The Administrative Assistant performs clerical tasks, disseminates important information throughout the organization to staff members, and compiles press releases. The Assistant also is the gatekeeper to who has access to the Executive Director.

Program Managers have the authority to direct staff members in carrying out the purpose of the organization. Program managers set the short term goals for their program. They use their expertise and professional skills to determine how case managers should develop treatment plans for clients' needs.

Case Managers carries out the service provision process. Case managers work closely with clients and implement treatment plans relevant to their needs and to the program.

Volunteers/Outreach Assistants assist each program managers in everyday routines and tasks. These are the trench workers; they disseminate information regarding services directly to the community. In addition, volunteers and assistants serve as symbols of The Caribbean Service Center's commitment to building and empowering the community. Many of these assistants are former clients and/or residents in the Caribbean community, looking to contribute to the organization's efforts while building work related skills.

Demographic Information

Below is Table 1 and Figures 1-5. Demographic information presented can be found in New York City Department of Planning's Report, The Newest New Yorkers, Analysis of Immigration, 1990 and 2000 Reports; Annual Immigrant Tape Files, U.S. Immigration and Naturalization Services 1970-2000.

Table 1: Total and Foreign-born Population, New York City and Boroughs, 1990-2000

	1990		2000		Change 1990-2000	
	Number	%	Number	%	Number	%
NYC Total Population	7,322,564	100.0	8,008,278	100.0	685,714	9.4
Foreign-born	2,082,931	28.4	2,871,032	35.9	788,102	37.8
Bronx Total Population	1,203,789	100.0	1,332,650	100.0	128,861	10.7
Foreign-born	274,793	22.8	385,827	29.0	111,034	40.4
Brooklyn Total Population	2,300,664	100.0	2,465,323	100.0	164,662	7.2
Foreign-born	672,569	29.2	931,769	37.8	259,200	38.5
Manhattan Total Population	1,487,538	100.0	1,537,195	100.0	49,659	3.3
Foreign-born	383,866	25.8	452,440	29.4	68,574	17.9

Queens Total Population	1,951,598	100.0	2,229,379	100.0	277,781	14.2
Foreign-born	707,153	36.2	1,028,339	46.1	321,186	45.4
Staten Island Total Population	378,977	100.0	443,728	100.0	64,751	17.1
Foreign	44,650	11.8	72,657	16.4	28,107	63.1

Figure 1 Map of Brooklyn, Copyright 1996

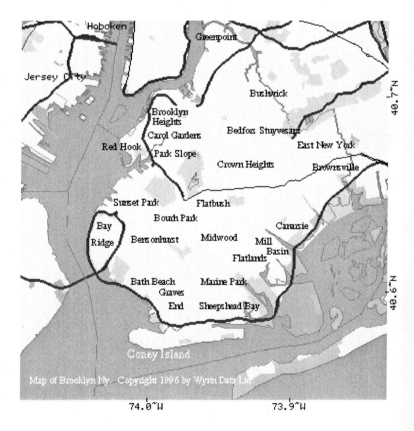

Figure 2 Distribution of Population by Nativity, New York City and United States, 2000

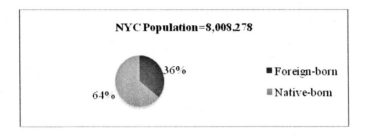

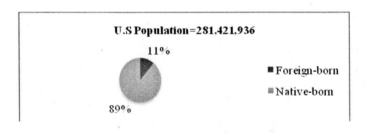

Figure 3 Areas of Origin of the Foreign-born Population, NYC and the United States, 2000

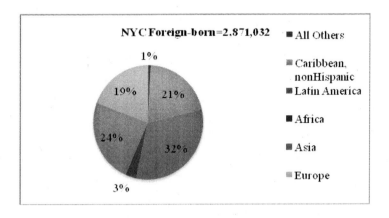

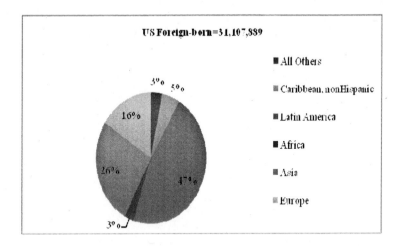

Figure 4 Total Populations by Nativity, New York City, 1990-2000

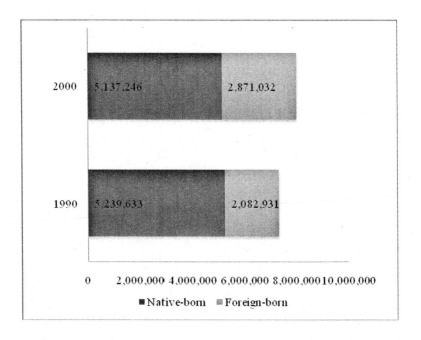

Figure 5 Foreign-born Populations by Area of Origin, New York City and Boroughs, 2000

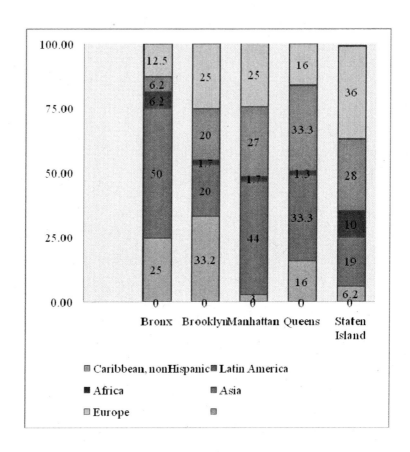

Figure 6 The Caribbean Service Center's Organizational Chart

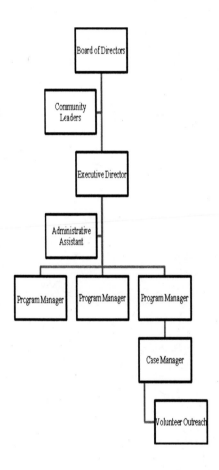

APPENDIX B

Listing of Participants

Name, Age, Sex	Education (Highest degree attained)	Role in organization	Ethnicity (Self Identification)	Immigrant Generation
Alex Acevedo, Early 40s, Male	Doctorate	Community Leader/ Activist	Dominican/ Caribbean/ Black/ Hispanic	1.5
Juan Carlos, Mid 50s, Male	Doctorate	Current Board Member	Panamanian/ Caribbean/ Black	1.5
Rita David, Early 50s, Female	Bachelor's	Community Leader	Panamanian/ Caribbean	1st
Dawn DeSousa, Mid-late 50s, Female	Doctorate	Founding Nurse/ Current Board Member	Jamaican/ West Indian/ Black	1st
Archibald Dubnet, Early 60s, Male	Doctorate	Current Board Member	Grenadian/ Caribbean	1st

Martha Espinosa, Late 30s, Female	Master's	Former Staff/ Current Board Member	Panamanian/ Black/ Hispanic	1.5
Sarah Flynn, Mid 20s, Female	High School/ Some college	Staff/ Domestic Violence Program	St. Lucian/ Black	1.5
Patricia Habeem, Late 30s, Female	Bachelor's	Staff/ Program Manager	Barbadian (Bajan)/ West Indian/ Black	1.5
Jose Henry, Late 30s, Male	Master's	Community Leader	Panamanian/ West Indian/ Black	1.5
Maria Hernandez Mid 40s, Female	Master's	Current Board Member	Jamaican/ West Indian	1st
Sharon Higgins, Mid 50s, Female	Master's	Founder/ Civil Servant	Jamaican/ West Indian/ Black	1st
Rasheeda Hines, Early 60s, Female	Doctorate	Community Leader/Civil Servant	Jamaican/ Black/ African American	1st

Christopher Jones, Mid 30s, Male	Bachelor's	Community Leader	Grenadian/ West Indian/ Black	1.5
Marshall Jones, Early 50s, Male	Doctorate	Current Board Member	Guyanese/ Caribbean/ Black	1st
Robert Lawson, Late 20s, Male	Bachelor's	Staff/Youth Outreach and Youth Services	Dominican/Black/ Latino	1.5
Charlene MacDonald Mid 50s, Female	Doctorate	Founding Nurse/ Current Board Member	St. Lucian/ Caribbean/ Black	1st
Wanda Martines, Mid 40s, Female	Doctorate	Staff/Legal Services	Anguillian/ Caribbean	1st
LaShawn Minks, Late 20s, Female	High school/ Some college	Staff/ Case manager for Asthma	Haitian/Black	1.5
Erica Parke, Early 40s, Female	Bachelor's	Community Leader	Anguillian/ Black	1st
Lenroy Reynolds, Late 50s, Male	Doctorate	Current Board Member	Trinidadian/ West Indian/ Caribbean/Black	1st

Victoria Samms, Late 50s, Female	High school/ Some college	Former Client and Current Staff/ General Case Manager	Jamaican/ West Indian	1st
Vanessa Smith, Late 50s, Female	Doctorate	Founding Nurse/ Current Board Member	Trinidadian/West Indian/ Black	1st
Veronica Stanley, Mid 30s, Female	Master's	Staff/ Maternal Health and WIC	African American	NA
Michelle Stevens, Mid 30s, Female	Master's	Community Leader	African American	NA
Clement Thomas, Mid 40s, Male	Master's	Community Leader	Haitian/ Black	1.5
Francois Toussaint, Late 40s, Male	Master's	Community Leader	Haitian	1.5
Tiffany Wells, Early 40s, Female	Master's	Staff/ Case Manager for Youth Services	Monserratian/ West Indian	1.5
Gary Whits, Early 60s, Male	Doctorate	Executive Director	Panamanian/ Caribbean/Black	1st
Shana Yugi, Mid 30s, Female	Bachelor's	Community Leader	Trinidadian/ Caribbean/ Black	1.5

Methodology and Description of Instrument

The analytic method and design employed in this case study attempted to reveal the relationship a central Brooklyn community-based organization has with its Caribbean immigrant clients and community members. The research's qualitative design was based on several research ethnographic principles: a blend of naturalistic principles (see Erlandson, Harris, Skipper, and Allen 1993; Hammersley 1998; Matza 1969), tenets of grounded theory (see Glaser and Strauss 1967; Lindlof 1995; Huberman and Miles 1998), and narrative analysis.

Naturalistic Principles. The aim of naturalism is to capture the character of naturally occurring behavior. This can only be achieved by first-hand contact with the behavior, not by inferences from what people do in artificial settings like experiments or from what they say in interviews about what they say they do elsewhere. This is the reason that ethnographers carry out research in natural settings that exist independently of the research process. The implication of studying behaviors in natural settings is that the researcher minimizes his or her effect on the behavior of the people being studied. The aim of naturalism is to increase the chances that what is discovered can be generalized to other similar settings (see Hammersley 1998).

Grounded Theory. Grounded theory is typically presented as an approach to doing qualitative research, in that its procedures are neither statistical nor quantitative in some other way. Grounded theory research begins by focusing on an area of study and gathers data from a variety of sources, including interviews and field observations. Once gathered, the data is analyzed using coding and theoretical sampling procedures. When this is done, theories are generated, with the help of interpretive procedures, before being finally written up and presented. This latter activity is an integral part of the research process. The general goal of grounded theory research is to construct theories in order to understand phenomena. A good grounded theory is one that is inductively derived from data, subjected to theoretical elaboration, and judged adequate to its domain with respect to a number of evaluative criteria. Although it has been developed and principally used within the field of sociology, grounded theory can be employed in a variety of different disciplines (see Glaser and Straus 1967).

Narrative Analysis. This analysis focuses on how the past shapes perceptions of the present, how the present shapes perceptions of the past, and how both shape perceptions of the future. The narrative taps into anecdotal information at the expense of all the usual social scientific considerations (representative sampling, operationalization of terms, use of controls, multivariate causal analysis). Narratives help the researcher gain entrance to the perspective of the subject in a way that deepens the researcher's understandings of what social life is all about. Narrative analysis is best used for exploratory purposes, sensitizing the researcher and illustrating aspects of theory. A common focus is the exploration of ethical, moral, and cultural ambiguities. Employing naturalistic research principals (relying on the first-hand experiences of those in the study to present a portrait of life as understood by them) with grounded theory is a way to identify how participants make meaning of the social world around them. The emphasis is on using narratives of participants' experiences that are faithful to their self-understandings and that illuminate their practices and negotiations in everyday life. This blend of naturalistic principles, grounded theory, and narrative analysis is well suited for an organizational study such as this one.

Research Process

In several cases, I met with participants more than once before conducting an interview in order to set participants at ease and to establish good rapport. Interviews were conducted in English either at The Caribbean Service Center, the participant's home or over the telephone, and depending on the participants' preference and availability. Interviews lasted between one half-hour and two hours. Using a template of semi-structured questions, participants discussed a range of issues, including but not limited to, specific examples and accounts of their perceptions, the challenges and concerns the community faces, The Caribbean Service Center and its role in community activism, local and organizational political activities, personal and community cultural beliefs, sense of identity, and personal migratory and settlement history. Interviews were tape recorded, in addition, extensive field notes were taken during and after each interview.

Data collection also included participant observation of various meeting forums. Specifically, program meetings and sporadic meetings between managers, staff, and the director as well as small, local events were observed as a way to explore inter-program and community interaction. Finally, observations were made by studying daily organizational activities and by attending an annual Caribbean American festival supported by New York City's Department of City Planning and Mayoral cabinets, and The Caribbean Service Center's affiliated members and clients.

It must be noted, however, that none of the participants in the study were clients. Although some of the participants disclosed they were former clients, the sample did not include current clients. Given the sensitive nature of clients' cases, I feared clients' voluntary disclosure of personal information (e.g., their citizen status-whether legal or illegal) may raise specific immigration issues; therefore, I excluded current clients. Despite this limitation, clients' perspectives are included in this research but only through more informal field note observation and personal conversations I had with clients that were not recorded.

Data Coding and Theme Development

Part of conducting a qualitative analysis on immigrants' ethnic identity construction and assertions within organizations is to allow the discovery of themes and sub-themes to reveal themselves from the interview data and then generate analyses that grow out of the participants' experiences. For this case study narratives were analyzed using thematic categories or codes pertaining to concepts of race and community politics, race and ethnic identity, immigrant perceptions, community empowerment, and migration, to name a few.

Using qualitative data analysis software, NUDIST (N6), portions of each document that pertained to each theme were coded and compared with all other coded portions of other narratives. From these highlighted themes, sub-themes were also formulated and examined. Observations and field notes were analyzed and coded as well. The themes and sub-themes that emerged from the narratives also focus on staff, directors, and community members' perceptions of Caribbean immigrant participation in central Brooklyn, New York. Perceptions reflect the staffs' daily experiences of delivering of health and social services to Caribbean immigrants, 1.5 and second generation Caribbean Americans, and African Americans in the community. Prominent issues that were examined include how the organization designs and delivers services to their Black ethnic, immigrant clientele; how staff negotiate and assert their own racial and ethnic identity in relation to their clients, community members, and other staff; and, how they perceive the organization should relate to state and federally-determined program requirements in light of the organization's constraint of politically mobilizing the community.

Advantages and Shortcomings faced in the field

Conducting an organizational analysis on the activities of The Caribbean Service Center was complex. There are, however, many factors to consider including fieldwork preparation, the researcher's role or behavior in the field, and problems and unexpected events that make this type of research more complicated than simply making open-ended observations. During my preliminary investigations of The Caribbean Service Center, I talked with the Executive Director and staff about the organization, its history, and workplace setting as well as set-up informal but brief visits to The Caribbean Service Center. Ultimately, I gained the trust and permission from the Director to conduct the research.

The trust that developed was, in large part, influenced by two personal factors. First, the research agenda and topic were of personal interest to the current Executive Director. The Executive Director conducted similar research in the community thirty years ago during the establishment of The Caribbean Service Center. The Executive

Director thought this case study could reveal interesting elements about the community and its changes since the inception of the community-based organization. Second, my informal connections to politically active United States' Caribbean consular agents affirmed my status as a Caribbean-identified researcher and as an insider to the Caribbean American community because these agents were able to personally vouch for me to the organization's Executive Director and program managers. With these two factors, I was able to gain access to The Caribbean Service Center's records, fiscal reports, and its staff.

To have a deeper understanding of the role The Caribbean Service Center has in the community, this organizational study also needed the perspectives of The Caribbean Service Center's Board members and affiliated community leaders, including local politicians. Because these individuals assist the community-based organization in achieving its mission and goals, adding their perspectives provided insight as to what they think the issues the Caribbean community face as well as The Caribbean Service Center's role in remedying these issues. I realized quickly that The Caribbean Service Center's Executive Director was the gatekeeper to my meeting members of the Board and local leaders. The Executive Director has personal relationships and correspondences with these affiliated members of The Caribbean Service Center and was able to exercise a certain level of control over my access to these politicians and avenues of opportunity to meet them. As a way to gain access to these affiliated members, I joined The Caribbean Service Center's Caribbean graduate student internship program.

By participating in the organization, I was able to shift my role from complete observer to a participant observer. As a complete observer, I watched how staff members interacted with co-workers and clients as well as conducted interviews that were formal and in bounded settings out of earshot of other people. As a participant observer, I worked alongside the staff and shared personal characteristics of myself as a way to relate to them. In both roles, I had to draw on shared interests and cultural experiences, engage in relevant activities, and develop some new interests that, I believed, would facilitate my interviews and interaction. Shifting my role from observer to participant observer was critical to understanding how individuals think and behave in certain settings. Conducting interviews and making observations alone, do not provide access to the cognitive and attitudinal understanding of an individual's behavior in an organizational setting. Being a participant observer helped me to understand how participants would behave in other circumstances different from a traditional interview setting.

The various roles I played, as Erving Goffman's (1959) abstract distinction between front stage and backstage suggests, allowed me to sufficiently use my interest in sociology, race, and Caribbean studies to add legitimacy to my role as a Caribbean American research intern and to the kinds of questions I asked about the community-based organization and the community. A concern throughout the ethnographic process was to avoid deceiving participants. Keeping my intentions as overt as possible, I often volunteered information about my work in Boston, Massachusetts, and answered questions about the case study. Participants seemed convinced of my intentions and often volunteered personal information about themselves, which they thought would be of interest to a participant observer.

As part of the data collection and analysis process, I noticed that the interpretation and accounts produced from interviews and research inevitably reflected the socio-historical position of both the respondents and myself. To a certain extent, I understood my own socio-historical location as a daughter of Caribbean immigrants, raised in Brooklyn, with an interest in the community I grew up in. I gained access to my interview sample by working closely with The Caribbean Service Center. To many of my respondents, I was seen as an insider in the organization as well as an insider in the Caribbean immigrant community. My interest in the community and shared Caribbean values conferred upon my respondents my insider position. Being an insider was an advantage since it allowed respondents to reveal more of themselves and their political stance on issues than would otherwise be the case. In that respect, I developed an understanding or an intuitive sense of the issues presented by respondents.

The danger of having an insider perspective is that the research runs the risk of presenting information that is distorted and lacks enough social distance for critical analyses to take place. Hence, I tried to minimize my political discussions during strategy sessions and allowed respondents to speak at length about their various personal and political experiences. In practical terms, the ethnographic methodology allowed me to see the context of the social and political world and the meaning systems negotiated and constructed in and through relationships more closely, thus informing my understanding of relationships under study.

In fact, using ethnography as a methodology to examine a system such as a community-based organization and the community it serves, including the relationship between the community-based organization and its racial-ethnic clients can prove valuable. The strength of the ethnography is its capacity to help researchers gain a rich understanding of a highly localized social phenomenon that would be difficult to obtain from other methods. The researcher can potentially identify linkages between society and individuals within various systems and settings (Rizzo and Corsaro 1995; Shadish 1995). By using this methodology, I was able to generate findings that can be applicable to other organizational and community studies. In particular, variability of research findings can be applied and developed into generalizable claims, which later can be used to develop more macro-approaches in the field. Ethnographic research and its ability to construct generalizable claims from highly localized circumstances (i.e., with particular people at a specific time using a small set of observations) can be an invaluable tool in the quest of knowledge on a social phenomena.

Although I may have operated from the standpoint of an insider I also faced several constraints as an outsider. My status as a Caribbean research intern, in many ways, inferred a low status position among staff members at The Caribbean Service Center. Initially, it was unclear to the staff what my role was at The Caribbean Service Center. Many realized that I attended various organizational meetings more than the typical intern who is responsible for assisting staff members with filing, photocopying, and daily administrative tasks. Many recognized that I did not have the power or privileges of regular staff members. After my initial interviews with staff members, some staff disclosed that they thought I was part of the Executive Director's team to gain inside information on staff member's actions and thoughts. A few staff members also believed that if they did not speak with me, their jobs and rapport with the Executive Director was in danger. In taking these perceptions into consideration, my low status and perceived alliance to the Executive Director were initial hindrances to me gaining the trust of staff. Fortunately, because The Caribbean Service Center's staff works closely together and often spoke of my presence in the organization, staff members shared their positive interactions with me to one another. After conversations with their co-workers, many staff members disclosed that they were a lot more comfortable with the idea of speaking with me about the research I was conducting on the organization and the Caribbean community.

An interesting obstacle in conducting a qualitative organizational analysis is the "politics of doing ethnographies" (Warnke 1987). The politics of ethnographies that focus on organizations and communities is always affected by social values and always have political consequences for the organization, its workers, and the research participants. Political implications or consequences of the research arise when the researcher uncovers information that was once known to few within the organization or by making public what had formerly been private.

By exploring the ethnic identity assertions of Caribbeans within the context of a community-based organization and the greater local politics, a strategy of this research is to bring attention to the perpetuation of racial ideologies that persist toward racial-ethnic, immigrants and to put pressure on those concerned with racial-ethnic and immigrant communities to actively address the problems that continue to plague these communities. I am convinced that the methodology used to uncover the influences community-based organizations have in the lives and ethnic identity construction of Caribbean immigrants will shed light on how much race and immigrant status shapes the lives and experiences of those defined racially as Black in American society.

Detailed Description of Programming and Services

Maternal and Child Health

1. *Brownsville Women and Infant Child Program*: Targets high risk, low income women in the Brownsville area of Brooklyn who have received little or no prenatal care, and seeks to coordinate services through case management.

2. *Brownsville Healthy Start Program*: Provides pre-conceptional case management, as well as moderate risk prenatal case management and referral services to pregnant and parenting families. Program also provides outreach and client education.

3. *Community Health Worker Program*: Provides prenatal case management and referral services to pregnant and parenting families, particularly in Far Rockaway, Queens.

4. *CHP/FHP –Child Health Plus/ Medicaid/WIC Facilitated Enrollment Initiative*: Provides facilitated enrollment into Child Health Plus or Medicaid for children under 19 years old. It also facilitates enrollment of adults into Family Health Plus, who are not qualified for Medicaid.

5. *Women, Infants and Children (WIC) Nutrition Program*: Provides nutrition counseling and food coupons to infants, children and pregnant/parenting women with children 5 years of age and younger.

6. *Comprehensive Prenatal-Perinatal Services Network of Brooklyn (CPPSN):* Through network involvement, members strategically plan goals focused to contribute to the reduction of low birth-weight and infant mortality rates by providing leadership that will strengthen collaboration among prenatal/perinatal providers, facilitate improved service delivery, and collect utilization and outcome data.

7. *Well Child Project:* Provides home visits and education for hard-to-reach clients in an effort to ensure managed care for children, including compliance of immunizations and regular preventive doctors visits.

8. *Immigrant Women Health Program:* Provides information, advocacy and referral services to immigrant women in need of accessing immigration, health and social support services.

HIV/AIDS Education and Case Management Program

HIV/AIDS Education and Case Management Program: Provides community outreach, education and case management services to HIV infected or affected individuals. The program also provides technical support, assistance and training to other providers of AIDS/HIV services.

Environmental Health

Asthma Educational Case Management Program: Provides home visits, education, case management and referral services.

Adolescent Health

Teen Abstinence Educational Program: The Caribbean Service Center's "PHAT" (Promoting Health and Abstinence Education Among Teens) program provides peer educators and parent advocates to promote the delay of sexual activity and foster healthy development for adolescents. The program works with adolescents ages 10-19 with a specific focus on children between the ages of 10 and 14.

Domestic Violence

The Caribbean Service Center provides on-site domestic violence counseling, case management, referral, and advocacy services.

Immigration

The Immigration Program has a multi-lingual, professional staff consisting of attorneys, immigration counselors and social workers to provide social support and immigration-related services, and represent clients at immigration hearings. In addition to providing the following services, the program is also responsible for conducting training seminars and operating a Speaker's Bureau with expert speakers on immigration related issues.

1. *Family Unification*: Provides legal counseling, support and educational services designed to foster family unification and help families access needed services, adjust to their environment, and resolve immigration problems.
2. *Citizenship*: Assists immigrants in becoming American Citizens. The Caribbean Service Center also is a citizenship test site for the Educational Testing Services.
3. *Legal Defense*: Provides legal services representing clients in Immigration Court.
4. *Immigrant Rights*: Initiates, endorses, develops, supports and provides programs designed to protect the rights of immigrants.

Primary Care

The Caribbean Service Center operates the Caribbean American Family Health Center (CAFHC) in partnership with Lutheran Medical Center and Sunset Park Family Health Center Network. CAFHC provides OB/GYN, Pediatrics, Internal Medicine and Family Practice Services.

Other Ancillary Programs

1. *International*: Conducts and participates in international conferences and field tours to study public health systems, and foster technology transfer and cross-cultural education.

2. *Cross-Cultural Health*: Conducts interdisciplinary studies and activities addressing cross-cultural health issues.

3. *Volunteer/Graduate Student Internship*: Offers individuals an opportunity to gain professional experience and make invaluable community service contributions.

4. *Conference/Seminars*: Addresses health, immigration, and socio-economic issues.

5. *Youth Services*: Designed to provide adolescents with basic work experience and skills development.

6. *Special Events*: Sponsors, "And Still They Rise," and "Laureates of Health Care" Benefit receptions to recognize outstanding leaders.

7. *Advocacy*: Conducts research, publishes reports, operates a Speakers Bureau, and testifies at public hearings.

8. *Management Support and Technical Assistance*: Provides management support and technical assistance to providers serving ethnic, immigrant and culturally diverse populations.

REFERENCES

Abrams, W. (1975). *Alternatives in community mental health*. Boston, Massachusetts: Beacon.

Abroms, L.C. and Maibach, E. (2008). The effectiveness of mass communication to change public behavior. *Annual Review of Public Health, 29*: 219-234.

Ahrne, G. (1993). *Social organizations*. London, England: Sage Publishing.

Alba, R. and Nee, V. (1995). The assimilation of immigrant groups: concept, theory and evidence." Social Science Research Council Conference Presentation (January 18—21) *Becoming American/ America Becoming: International Migration to the United States*. Sanibel, Florida.

Alba, R. and Nee, V. (1997). Rethinking assimilation theory for a new era of immigration. *International Migration Review. 31*(4): 826-874.

Alba, R. and Nee, V. (2005). *Remaking the American mainstream: assimilation and contemporary immigration*. Cambridge, Massachusetts: Harvard University Press.

Aldrich, H. (1999).*Organizations evolving*. Thousand Oaks, California: Sage Publications.

Anderson, B. (1983). *Imagined communities: reflections on the origin and spread of nationalism*. London, England: Verso.

Anderson, B., and Isaacs, A. (2007). Simply not there: the impact of international migration of nurses and midwives- perspectives from Guyana. *Journal of Midwifery and Women's Health, 52*(4):392–97.

Basch, L. (1987). "The Vincentians and Grenadians: the role of voluntary associations in immigrant adaptation to New York City." In Foner (Eds.), *New Immigrants in New York*. New York, New York: Columbia University Press.

Basch, L. (1992). The politics of Caribbeanization: Vincentians and Grenadians in New York." In Sutton and Chaney (Eds.), *Caribbean Life in New York City* (pp. 147-166). New York, New York: Center of Migration Studies.

Bassey, M. (2007). The place of group consciousness in black autobiographical narratives. *Journal of African American Studies, 11* (3/4): 214-224.

Bell, D. (2004). *Silent covenants: brown v. board of education and the unfulfilled hopes for racial reform.* New York, New York: Oxford University Press.

Benson, J. (2006). Exploring the racial identities of black immigrants in the United States. *Sociological Forum, 21*(2):219-243.

Berry, J., and Phinney, J. (2006). *Immigrant youth in cultural transition: acculturation, identity, and adaptation across national contexts.* Mahwah, New Jersey: Lawrence Erlbaum Associates Inc., Publishers.

Biko, S. (1971). Defining black consciousness. Excerpts From Steve Biko's (August 28, 1971) Address at a Black Theology Seminar in Pietermaritzburg.

Breines, W. (1989). *Community and organization in the new left, 1962-1968.* New Brunswick, New Jersey: Rutgers University Press.

Brettell, C. (2000). Urban history, urban anthropology, and the study of migrants in cities. *Cities and Society, 12*: 129-138.

Briggs, V. (1984). *Immigration policy and the American labor force.* Baltimore, Maryland: Johns Hopkins University Press.

Brodkin, K. (1998). *How Jews became white folks and what that says about race in America.* New Brunswick, New Jersey: Rutgers University Press.

Brown, K. McCarthy. (1991). *Mama Lola: a vodou priestess in Brooklyn.* Berkeley, California: University of California Press.

Brubaker, R. (2009). Ethnicity, race, and nationalism. *Annual Review of Sociology, 35*: 21-42.

Bryce-Laporte, R. (1972). Black immigrants: the experience of invisibility and inequality. *Journal of Black Studies, 3*: 29-56.

Bryce-Laporte, R. (1979). Introduction: New York City and the new Caribbean immigration: a contextual statement. *International Migration Review, 13* (2):214-234.

Burns, T and Stalker, G. (1994). *The management of innovation.* New York, New York: Oxford University Press.

Caro, R. (1974). *The power broker: Robert Moses and the fall of New York.* New York, New York: Knopf.

Cohen, J. (1985). Strategy or identity? new theoretical paradigms and contemporary social movements. *Social Research, 52*, 663-716.

Cordero-Guzman, H., Grosfoguel, R., and Smith, R. (2001). *Migration, transnationalism, and race in a changing New York.* Philadelphia, Pennsylvania: Temple University Press.

Cornell, S. and Hartmann, D. (1998). *Ethnicity and race: making identities in a changing world*. Thousand Oaks, California: Pine Forge.

Crowder, K., and Tedrow, L. (2001). West Indians and the residential landscape of NewYork." In Foner (Ed.), *Islands in the city: West Indian migration to New York*, Berkeley, California: University of California Press.

Davis, J.F. (1991). *Who is black? one nation's definition*. University Park, Pennsylvania: University of Pennsylvania Press.

Dawson, M. (1994) *Behind the mule*. Princeton, New Jersey: Princeton University Press.

Dion, K., K. Dion, and Wang-Ping Pak, A. (1992). Personality-based hardiness as a buffer for discrimination-related stress in members of Toronto's chinese community. *Canadian Journal of Behavioral Science, 24*: 517-536.

Dolan, J. (1975). *The immigrant church: New York's Irish and German Catholics, 1815-1865*. Baltimore, Maryland: Johns Hopkins University Press.

Dominquez, J. (1991). Immigration as foreign policy in United States-Latin American relations." In *Immigration and U.S. Foreign Policy*. Boulder, Colorado: West View Press.

Duany, J. (1998). Reconstructing racial identity: ethnicity, color, and class among Dominicans in the United States and Puerto Rico. *Latin American Perspectives, 25*:147-172.

Dubois, C. (2003). *Images of West Indian Immigrants in Mass Media: The Struggle for a Positive Ethnic Reputation*. El Paso, Texas: LFB Scholarly Publishing.

Dunst, C., C. Trivette, and. Deal, A. (1988). *Enabling and empowering families*. Cambridge, Massachusetts: Brookline Books.

Eames, E. and Goode, J.G. (1977). *Anthropology of the city: an introduction to urban anthropology*. Upper Saddle River, New Jersey: Prentice Hall.

Edmonston, B. and Passel, J. (1994). *Immigration and ethnicity: the integration of America's newest arrivals*. District of Columbia: Urban Institute Press.

Emerson, R. (1962). Power-dependence relations. *American Sociological Review, 27*(1): 31-40.

Erie, S. P. (1988). *Rainbow's end: Irish-Americans and the dilemmas of urban machine politics, 1840-1985*. Berkeley, California: University of California Press.

Erlandson, D. A., Harris, E. L., Skipper, B. L., and Allen, S. D. (1993). *Doing naturalistic inquiry: a guide to methods*. Thousand Oaks, California: Sage Publications.

Espiritu, Y. (1992). *Asian American pan-ethnicity: bridging institutions and identities*. Philadelphia, Pennsylvania: Temple University Press.

Etzioni, D. (1964). *Modern organizations*. Upper Saddle River, New Jersey: Prentice Hall.

Ferree, Myra and Hess, B. (1994). *Controversy and coalition*. Woodbridge, Connecticut: Twayne Publishers.

Foner, N. (1987). The Jamaicans: race and ethnicity among migrants in New York City." In Foner (Eds.), *New Immigrants in New York*. New York, New York: Columbia University Press.

Foner, N. (2001). *Islands in the city*. Berkeley, California: University of California Press.

Foster-Fishman, P., Cantillon D., Pierce S., and Van Egeren L. (2007). Building an active citizenry: the role of neighborhood problems, readiness, and capacity for change. *American Journal of Community Psychology, 39*(1 /2):91–106.

Foster, R. (1967). *Brooklyn is America*. Brooklyn, New York: AMS Press.

Fuchs, L. (1956). *The political behavior of Jews*. Glencoe, Illinois: The Free Press.

Garvey, M. (1921/1974). Up you mighty race. Excerpt from UNIA speech. In Clarke (Ed.,), *Marcus Garvey and the Vision of Africa* (July 1921). New York, New York: Random House.

Gerth, H. and Wright Mills, C. (1958). *From Max Weber: Essays in Sociology*. New York, New York: Oxford University Press.

Gilliam, F.D. and Kaufman, K.M. (1998). Is there an empowerment life cycle?: long-term black empowerment and its influence on voter participation. *Urban Affairs Review, 33* (6): 741-767.

Glaser, B.G., and Strauss, A.L. (1967). *The Discovery of grounded theory: strategies for qualitative research*. Chicago, Illinois: Aldine.

Glazer, N. and Moynihan, D.P. (1963). *Beyond the melting pot: the Negroes, Puerto ricans, Jews, Italians, and Irish of New York*. Cambridge, Massachusetts: MIT Press.

Glazer, N. and Moynihan, D.P. (1975). Introduction. In Glazer and Moynihan (Eds). *Ethnicity: Theory and Experience*. Cambridge, Massachusetts: Harvard University Press.

Gleason, P. (1968). An immigrant group's interest in progressive reform: the case of the German-American Catholics. *American Historical Review*, *73*(2):367-379.

Gleason, P. (1968). *The conservative reformers: German-American Catholics and the social order.* Notre Dame, Indiana: Notre Dame University Press.

Glick-Schiller, N., Basch, L., and Szanton-Blanc, C. (1992). *Towards a transnational perspective on migration: race, class, ethnicity, and nationalism reconsidered.* New York, New York: New York Academy of Sciences.

Goffman, E. (1959). *The presentation of self in everyday life.* New York, New York: Doubleday.

Gordon, M. (1964). *Assimilation in American life.* New York, New York: Oxford University Press.

Greenberg, C. (1997). Negotiating Coalition: Black and Jewish Civil Rights Agencies in the 20th Century. In Salzman & West (Eds.), *Struggles in the Promised Land: Toward a History of Black-Jewish Relations in the United States* (pp. 153-176). New York, New York: Oxford University Press.

Gurin, P., Hatchett, S.,and Jackson, J.S.(1989). *Hope and independence: blacks' response to electoral and party politics.* New York, New York: Russell Sage.

Gutierrez, R.A. and Jones, C. (1995). *Rethinking the borderlands.* Berkeley, California: University of California Press.

Hammersley, M. (1998). *Reading ethnographic research: a critical guide.* London, England: Longman.

Handlin, O. (1959). *Immigration as a factor in American history.* Upper Saddle River, New Jersey: Prentice Hall.

Handlin, O. (1973). *The uprooted: the epic story of the great migration that made the American people.* Boston, Massachusetts: Little, Brown.

Heesacker, M. and Carroll, TA. (1997). Identifying and solving impediments to the social and counseling psychology interface. *The Counseling Psychologist*, *25*, 171-179.

Hendricks, G. (1974). *The Dominican Diaspora: from the Dominican Republic to New York City: villagers in transition.* New York, New York: Columbia University, Teachers College Press.

Herring, RD. (1996). *Counseling diverse ethnic youth.* Fort Worth, Texas: Harcourt Brace.

Hill Collins, P. (2000). *Black feminist thought.* New York, New York: Routledge.

Ho, C. (1991). *Salt-water Trinnies: Afro-Trinidadian immigrant networks and non-assimilation in Los Angeles*. Brooklyn, New York: AMS Press.

Hodges, V., Burwell, Y., and Ortega, D. (1998). Empowering families. In. Gutierrez, Parsons, and Cox (Eds.), *Empowerment in social work practice: a sourcebook* (pp. 146-162). New York, New York: Brooks-Cole.

Hogg, M., and Terry, D. (2000). Social identity and self-categorization processes in organizational contexts. *Academy of Management Review, 25* (1): 121-140.

Howe, M. (1990). *Immigration in New York state: impact and issues*. Albany, New York: NYS Department of Social Services.

Huberman, M., and Miles, M. (1998). Data management and analysis methods." In Denzin and Lincoln (Eds.,) *Collecting and Interpreting Qualitative Materials* (pp. 179-210). Thousand Oaks, California: Sage.

Hume, S. (2008). Ethnic and national identities of Africans in the U.S. *Geographical Review, 98*(4): 496-512.

Hurston, Zora Neal. (1942/2006). *Dust tracks on a road: an autobiography*. New York, New York: Modern Classics.

Iglehardt, A. and Becerra, R. (1995). *Social services and the ethnic community*. Boston, Massachusetts: Allyn and Bacon.

Itzigsohn, J., and Dore-Cabral, C. (2000). The formation of Latino and Latina pan-ethnic identities. In Foner and Fredrickson (Eds.,), *Not Just Black and White: Historical and Contemporary Perspectives on Immigration, Race, and Ethnicity in the United States* (pp 197-216). New York, New York: Russell Sage Foundation.

INS Bureau and New York City Planning Commission.(1970-2000). *Annual Reports*.

Jackson, P. and Lassiter S. (2001). Self-esteem and race. In Ownes, Stryker, and Goodman (Eds.,) *Extending Self-esteem Theory in Research*. London, England: Cambridge University Press.

Jenkins, C.J. and Perrow C. (1977). Insurgency of the powerless: farm workers movement, 1942-1972. *American Sociological Review, 42*: 249-268.

Jenkins, S. (1988). Introduction: immigration, ethnic associations, and social services. In Jenkins (Ed.,) *Contesting the limits of Political Participation: Latinos and black African Migrant Workers*. New York, New York: Routledge.

Jones, A. (2008) A silent but mighty river: the costs of women's economic migration. *Signs: Journal of Women in Culture and Society, 33* (4):761-769.

Kasinitz, P. and Vickerman, M. (2001). Ethnic niches and racial traps: Jamaicans in the New York regional economy." In Cordero Guzman, Grosfoguel, and Smith (Eds.,) *Migration, Transnationalism, and Race in a Changing New York*. Philadelphia, Pennsylvania: Temple University Press.

Kasinitz, P. (1992). *Caribbean New York: black immigrants and the politics of race*. Ithaca, New York: Cornel University Press.

Kast and Ronsenzweig (1973). *Contingency view of organization and management*. Chicago, Illinois: Science Research Association, Inc.

Kazal, R. (1995). Revisiting assimilation: the rise, fall, and reprisal of a concept in American ethnic history. *American Historical Review, 100*:460-472.

Keely, C. (1990). Immigration in the interwar period. In Keely (Ed.,) *Immigration and U.S. Foreign Policy* (pp 42-56). Boulder, Colorado: West View Press.

Klevan, M. (1990). *The West Indian Americans*. New York, New York: Chelsea House Publications.

Kieffer, C. (1984). Citizen empowerment: a developmental perspective. In Rappaport, Swift, and Hess (Eds.), *Studies in empowerment: steps toward understanding and action* (pp. 9-36). New York, New York: Haworth Press.

Kim, Y. (1994). The Correlation between religiosity and assimilation of first-generation Korean Immigrants in the Chicago Metropolitan Region. (Doctoral Dissertation, Loyola University of Chicago, 1994). Chicago, Illinois: Dissertation Archives. .

Kim, K..C (1991). The religious participation of Korean immigrants in the United States. *Journal for the Scientific Study of Religion. 29*(1): 19-35.

Kirwan Institute for the Study of Race and Ethnicity (2009). African American-immigrant alliance building. *Special Report, May*.

Kivisto, P. (2005). *Incorporating diversity: rethinking assimilation in a multicultural age*. Boulder, Colorado: Paradigm Publishers.

Kraly, E.P. (1987). U.S immigration policy and immigrant populations of New York. In Foner (Ed.,) *New Immigrants in New York City* (pp 35-78). New York, New York: Columbia University Press.

Kwon, V.H (1997). The structure and functions of cell group ministry in a Korean Christian church. *Journal for the Scientific Study of Religion, 36*:247-256.

Laguerre, M. (1984). *American odyssey: Haitians in New York City*. Ithaca, New York: Cornell University Press.

Lawrence, PR., and Lorsch, J. (1967). *Organization and environment.* Cambridge, Massachusetts: Harvard University Press.

Lee, J. (1994). *The empowerment approach to social work practice.* New York, New York: Columbia University Press.

Levitt, P. (1998). Local-level global religion: the case of U.S.-Dominican migration. *Journal for the Scientific Study of Religion, 37* (1):74-89.

Levitt, P. (2001). *Transnational villagers.* Berkeley, California: University of California Press.

Levitt, P., and Jaworsky, B. (2007). Transnational migration studies: past developments and future trends. *Annual Review of Sociology, 33:* 129-156.

Lindlof, T. (1995). *Qualitative communication research methods.* Thousand Oaks, California: Sage.

Lissak, R. (1989). *Pluralism and progressives: hull house and the new immigration.* Chicago, Illinois: University of Chicago Press.

Litt, E. (1970). *Ethnic politics in America: beyond pluralism.* Glenview, Illinois: Scott Fresman.

Locke, D. (1997). *Increasing multicultural understanding.* Thousand Oaks, California: Sage.

Mackie, M. and Brinkerhoff, M.B. (1984). Measuring ethnic salience. *Canadian Ethnic Studies, 16:* 114-131.

Mana, A., Orr, E., Mana, Y. (2009). An integrated acculturation model of immigrants' social identity. *Journal of Social Psychology, 149* (4): 450-473.

Mangum, M. (2008). Testing competing explanations of black opinions on affirmative action. *Policy Studies Journal, 36*(3): 347-366.

March, J.G., and Simon, H. (1958). *Organizations.* New York, New York: Wiley.

Massey, D. and Denton, N. (1987). Trends in the residential segregation of blacks, Hispanics, and Asians, 1970-1980. *American Sociological Review, 487:*102-113.

Massey, D. (1994). *The new immigration and the meaning of ethnicity in the United States.* Albany, New York: American Diversity.

Matza, D. (1969). *Becoming deviant.* Upper Saddle River, New Jersey: Prentice Hall.

Melucci, A. (1985). The symbolic challenge of contemporary movements. *Social Research, 52:*789-816.

Melucci, A. (1996). *Challenging codes: collective action in the information age.* New York, New York: Cambridge University Press.

Menjívar, C. (1999). Religious institutions and transnationalism: a case study of catholic and evangelical Salvadoran immigrants. *International Journal of Politics, Culture and Society, 12* (4): 589-612.

Merton, R. (1996). *On social structure and science.* Chicago, Illinois: University of Chicago Press.

Minkoff, D. (1995). *Organizing for Equality: The Evolution of Women's and Racial and Ethnic Organizations in America, 1955-1985.* New Brunswick, New Jersey: Rutgers University Press.

McAdams, D. (1995). Initiator and spin-off movements: diffusion professes in protest cycles. In Traugott (ed.,) *Repertoires and Cycles of Collective Action.* Durham, North Carolina: Duke University Press.

McCarthy, J. and Zald, M. (1973). *The trend of social movements in America: professionalization and resource mobilization.* Englewood Cliffs, New Jersey: General Learning Press.

McClain, P., Johnson, J., Walton, E., and Watts, C. (2009). Group membership, group identity, and group consciousness: measures of racial identity in American politics. *Annual Review of Political Science, 12*: 471-485.

McGregor, D. (1960). *The human side of enterprise.* New York, New York: McGraw Hill.

McKay, C. (1922/2009). The tropics in New York. *Harlem shadows: the poems of Claude McKay.* Whitefish, Montana: Kessinger Publishing.

Moore, C. (1984, August 28). The Caribbean community and the quest for political power. *Caribbean News* (pp 1A).

Morawska, E. (1994). In defense of the assimilation model. *Journal of American Ethnic History, 13*: 76-87.

Myrdal, G. (1944). *An American dilemma.* New York, New York: Harper & Row.

Nelli, H. (1970). Italians in Chicago 1880-1930: a study on ethnic mobility. *Journal of American History, 58* (8): 776-778.

New York City Department of Planning (1970-2000). *The Newest New Yorkers: an analysis of immigration into New York City.* New York, New York: Department of Planning.

Obidinski, E. (1978). Methodological considerations in definition of ethnicity. *Ethnicity, 5*: 213-228.

Olwig, K.F. (1993). *Global culture, island identity: continuity and change in the afro-Caribbean community of Nevis.* New York, New York: Harwood Academic Publishers.

Omi, M. and Winant H. (1994). *Racial formation in the United States: from the 1960s to the 1990s, 2nd edition.* New York, New York: Routledge.

Orsi, R.A. (1985). *The Madonna of 115th Street: faith and community in Italian Harlem, 1880-1950.* New Haven, Connecticut: Yale University Press.

Padilla, F. (1986). Latino ethnicity in the city of Chicago. In Olzak and Nagel (eds.,) *Competitive Ethnic Relations.* New York, New York: Academic Press.

Padilla, F. (1985). *Latino ethnic consciousness: The case of Mexican Americans and Puerto Ricans in Chicago.* Notre Dame, Indiana: University of Notre Dame Press.

Papademetriou, D.G. (1983). *New immigrants to Brooklyn and Queens: policy implications with regard to housing.* New York, New York: Center for Migration Studies.

Park, E. (1950). *Race and culture.* Glencoe, Illinois: The Free Press.

Park, E. and Burgess, E. (1924). *Introduction to the science of sociology.* Chicago, Illinois: University of Chicago Press.

Parsons, R. J. (1991). Empowerment: purpose and practice principle in social work. *Social Work with Groups, 14*: 7-21.

Parsons, T. (1937). *The Structure of Social Action.* New York: McGraw Hill.

Phinney, S. (1991). Ethnic identity and self-esteem: a review and integration. *Hispanic Journal of Behavioral Sciences, 13*: 193-208.

Pickus, N. (1998). *Immigration and citizenship in the twenty-first century.* Lanham, Maryland: Bowman & Littlefield.

Piedra, LM., and Engstrom, D.W. (2009). Segmented assimilation theory and the life model: an integrated approach to understanding immigrants and their children. *Social Work, 54* (3): 270-277.

Portes, A. (1995). Children of immigrants: segmented assimilation and its determinants. In Portes (Ed.,), *The Economic Sociology of Immigration: Essays on Networks, Ethnicity, and Entrepreneurship.* New York, New York: Russell Sage Foundation.

Portes, A., .Guarnizo, L., and Landolt, P. (1999). The study of transnationalism: pitfalls and promise of an emergent research field. *Ethnic and Racial Studies, 22,* 6: 217-237.

Portes, A. and Bach, R. (1985). *Latin journey: Cuban and Mexican immigrants in the United States.* Berkeley, California: University of California Press.

Portes, A. and Grosfoguel, R. (1994). Caribbean Diasporas: migration and ethnic communities. *Annals of the American academy of political and social science, 536*: 48-69.

Portes, A. and Rumbaut, R. (1996). From immigrants to ethnics: identity, citizenship, and political participation. *Immigrant America: a portrait.* Berkeley, California: University of California Press.

Portes, A. and Rumbaut, R. (1990). *Immigrant America: a portrait*. Berkeley, California: University of California Press.

Portes, A. and Zhou, M. (1993). The new second generation: segmented assimilation and its variants among post-1965 immigrant youth. *Annals of the American Academy of Political and Social Science, 530*: 74-96.

Portes, A. and Zhou, M. (1992). Gaining the Upper Hand: Economic Mobility among Immigrant and Domestic minorities. *Racial and Ethnic Studies*, 15: 491-522.

Ravage, M. (1917). *An American in the Making*. NY: Harper.

Reinharz, S. (1992). *Feminist Methods in Social Research*. New York, New York: Oxford University Press.

Reissman, F. (1990). Restructuring help: A human services paradigm for the 1990s. *American Journal of Community Psychology*, 18, 221-230.

Rieder, J. (1995). Reflections on Crown Heights: interpretive dilemmas and Black-Jewish conflict. In Chanes (Ed.) *Anti-Semitism in America Today: Outspoken Experts Explode the Myths*. Secaucus, New Jersey: Carol Publishing Group.

Riesman, D., and Glazer, N. (1950). Criteria for political apathy. In Gouldner (Ed.), *Studies in Leadership* (pp. 505-559). New York, New York: Harper and Row.

Ringer, B., and Lawless, E., (1989). *Race, ethnicity, and society*. New York, New York: Routledge.

Rizzo, T. A. and Corsaro, W. A. (1995). Social support processes in early childhood friendship: a comparative study of ecological congruencies in enacted support. *American Journal of Community Psychology, 23*:389-417.

Rogers, R. (2001). Black like who? afro-Caribbean immigrants, African Americans, and the politics of group identity." In Foner (Ed.), *Islands in the city: West Indian migration to New York*. Berkeley, California: University of California Press.

Rogers, R. (2004). Race-based coalitions among minority groups: afro-caribbeans and African Americans in New York City. *Urban Affairs Review, 39* (3): 283-317.

Rogers, R. (2006). *Afro-Caribbean immigrants and the politics of incorporation: ethnicity, exception, or exit*. New York, New York: Cambridge University Press.

Rong, X., and Brown, F. (2002). Socialization, culture, and identities in educating black immigrant children: what educators need to know and do. *Education and Urban Society, 34*(2): 247-272.

Rong, X. Lang. and Fitchett, P. (2008). Socialization and identity transformation of black immigrant youth in the United States. *Theory into Practice, 47*: 35-42.

Rosenstein, C. (2006). *Cultural heritage organizations: nonprofits that support traditional, ethnic, folk, and noncommercial popular culture.* Washington, District of Columbia: The Urban Institute.

Rothschilds-Whitt, J. (1979). The collectivist organization: an alternative to national bureaucratic models. *American Sociological Review, 44*:509-527.

Rumbaut, R. (1994). The crucible within: ethnic identity, self-esteem, and segmented assimilation among children of immigrants. *International Migration Review, 28*: 748-794.

Rupp, L. and Taylor, V. (1999). Forging feminist identity in an international movement: a collective identity approach to twentieth-century feminism. *Signs, 24*: 363-386.

Shadish, W. R. (1995). The logic of generalization: five principles common to experiments and ethnographies. *American Journal of Community Psychology, 23* (3): 419-429.

Schenider, B., Brief, A., and Guzzo, R. (1996). Creating a climate and culture. *Organizational Dynamics, 24* (4): 7-19.

Sechzer and Ngang. (1991). United States immigration policy reform in the 1980s." In *Immigration and U.S. Foreign Policy.* Boulder, Colorado: West View Press.

Serpe, R. and Stryker, R. (1987). The construction of self and the reconstruction of social relationships. In Lawler and Markovsky (Eds.,) *Advances in Group Processes* (pp 41-66), *4.* Stamford, Connecticut: JAI Press.

Sleeper, J. (1990). *The Closest of Strangers: Liberalism and the Politics of Race in New York.* New York, New York: W.W. Norton.

Snow, D. and McAdams, D. (2001). Identity work processes in the context of social movements: clarifying the identity/ movement nexus." In Stryker, Owens, and White (Eds.,) *Self, Identity, and Social Movements* (pp 41-67). Minneapolis, Minnesota: University of Minnesota Press.

Solomon, B. (1987). Empowerment: social work in oppressed communities. *Journal of Social Work Practice, 2,* 79-91.

Solomon, B. (1976). *Black empowerment: Social work in oppressed communities.* New York, New York: Columbia University Press.

Stafford, W. (1996). Black civil society: fighting for a seat at the table. *Social Policy, 27*(2):11-18.

Staggenborg, S. (1998). Social movement communities and cycles of protest: the emergence and maintenance of a local women's movement. *Social Problems, 45(2)*:180-204.

Staples, L. (1990).Powerful ideas about empowerment. *Administration in Social Work, 14*: 29-42.

Stepick, A., Rey, T., and Mahler, S. (2009). *Churches and charity in the immigrant city: religion, immigration, and civic engagement in Miami.* New Brunswick, New Jersey: Rutgers University Press.

Su, C. (2009). We call ourselves by many names: storytelling and inter-minority coalition building. *Community Development Journal, Advance Access Online, April 15.*

Sue, D.W., and Sue, S. (1990). *Counseling the culturally different.* Hoboken, New Jersey: Wiley and Sons.

SUNY Downstate Medical Center. (2000). A *Community Report*. Brooklyn, New York: Archives.

Tajfel, H. (1974). Social Identity and Inter-group Behavior. *Social Science Information*, 13: 65-93.

Tarca, K. (2005). Colorblind in control: the risks of resisting difference amid demographic change. *Educational Studies, 38*(2): 99–120.

Tarrow, S. (1994). *Power in Movement: Social Movements, Collective Action and Politics.* New York: Cambridge University Press.

Tate, K. 1991. Black political participation in the 1984 and 1988 presidential elections. *American Political Science Review, 85*(4): 159-76.

Taylor, V. and Whittier, N. (1995). Analytical approaches to social movement culture: the culture of the women's movement." In Johnston and Klandermans (Eds.,), *Social Movements and Culture* (pp 163-187). Minneapolis, Minnesota: University of Minnesota Press.

Therborn, G. (2004). *Between sex and power: family in the world, 1900–2000.* New York, New York: Routledge

Thomas, WI. and Znaniecki, F. (1923). *The polish peasant in Poland and in America.* New York, New York: Knopf.

Tilly, C. (1979). Repertoires of contention in America and Great Britain." In Ferree and Martin (Eds.,) *The Dynamics of Social Movements.* Philadelphia, Pennsylvania: Temple University Press.

Tocqueville, A. (1969). *Democracy in America.* New York, New York: Anchor Books.

Traub, J. (1994). *City on a hill: testing the American dream at city college.* Reading, Massachusetts: Addison-Wesley.

Trickett, E. (2009). Community psychology: individuals and interventions in community context. *Annual Review of Psychology, 60*:395-419.

United States Bureau of the Census. 1990, 2000. Census of population. Washington, District of Columbia: United States Government.

United States Bureau of the Census. Immigrants and Naturalization Service, 1991a. Washington, District of Columbia: United States Government.

Valocchi, S. (2001). Individual identities, collective identities, and organizational structure. *Sociological Perspectives, 44* (4): 445-467.

Vickerman, M. (1994). The responses of West Indians to African Americans: distancing and identification. *Research in Race and Ethnic Relations, 7*:83-128.

Vickerman, M. (1999). *Cross currents: West Indian immigrants and race.* New York, New York: Oxford University Press.

Waldinger, R., and Fitzgerald, D. (2004). Transnationalism in question. *American Journal of Sociology, 109* (5): 1177-1196.

Wamsley,G., and Zald, M. (1973). *The political economy of public organizations.* Lanham, Maryland: Lexington Books.

Warner, R.S. (1993). Work in progress toward a new paradigm for the sociological study of religion in the United States. *American Journal of Sociology, 98*: 1044-1093.

Warner, R.S., and Wittner, J.G. (1998). *Gatherings in Diaspora: religious communities and the new immigration.* Philadelphia, PA: Temple University Press.

Warner, W.L. and Srole, L. (1945). *The social systems of American ethnic groups.* New Haven, Connecticut: Yale University Press.

Warnke, G. (1987). *Gadamer: hermeneutics, tradition, and reason.* Cambridge, Massachusetts: Polity Press.

Waters, M. (1994). Ethnic and racial Identities of second generation black immigrants in New York City. *International Migration Review, 28*: 795-820.

Waters, M. (1999). *Black identities: West Indian immigrant dreams and American realities.* Cambridge, Massachusetts: Harvard University Press/Russell Sage.

Weber, M. (1981). Bureaucracy. In Grusky and Miller (Eds.,) *The sociology of organizations, 2nd edition.* New York, New York: The Free Press.

West, C. (1993). *Race matters.* Boston, Massachusetts: Beacon

Wheeler, C. (1988). Alien eligibility for public benefits, parts 1 and 2. *Immigration Briefings.* (November). Washington, District of Columbia: Federal Publications, Inc.

White, C.L. and Burke, P.J., (1987). Ethnic role identity among black and white college students. *Sociological Perspectives, 30*: 310-331.

White, JL. and Parham, TA. (1990). *The psychology of blacks.* Englewood Cliff, New Jersey: Prentice Hall.

Williams,D.R., Gonzalez, H.M., Neighbors, H., Baser, R., and Jackson, J. S. (2007). The mental health of black Caribbean immigrants: results from the national survey of American life. *American Journal of Public Health, 97*: 52-59

Yoshikawa, H., and Way, N. (2008). From peers to policy: how broader social contexts influence the adaptation of children and youth in immigrant families. *New Directions for Child and Adolescent Development, 121*: 1-30.

Youssef, N. (1992). *The demographic of immigration: a socio-demographic profile of the foreign-born population in New York State.* New York, New York: Center for Migration Studies.

Yu, FT., and Kwan, DSM. (2008). Social construction of national identity: Taiwanese versus Chinese consciousness. *Social Identities, 14* (1):33-52.

Zald, M. (1970). Political economy: a framework for comparative Analysis. In Zald (Ed.,), *Power in Organizations* (pp 221-261). Nashville, Tennessee: Vanderbilt University Press.

Zephir, F. (1996). *Haitian immigrants in black America: a sociological and sociolinguistic portrait.* Westport, Connecticut: Bergin and Garvey.

Zhou, M. (1998). *Growing up American: the adaptation of adolescents in the United States.* New York, New York: Russell Sage Foundation.

INDEX

Abrams, 14
Abroms and Maibach, 39
Acculturation, 3, 6, 8
    scholarship on, 2
    process, 2
African American
    stigma of label, 4
African Americans
    American-born Blacks. *See*
        Blacks
Ahrne, 13
Alba and Nee, 2, 5, 11
Aldrich, 13, 44, 45, 75, 128
Alexis de Tocqueville. *See* Bell
American politics
    racial barriers to, 127
American racism, 117, 121, 131,
    142, 143
Anderson and Isaacs, 48, 143
Anti-Blackness
    overt and covert, 117
Apathy, 112, 113, 120-122, 124
Assimilation, 6, 11, 24, 82, 106,
    136
        classic definition of. *See*
            Park and Burgess
        classic European model, 3

and ethnic enclaves and
    social networks, 5
segmented, 5, 12, 15, 106,
    135, 141
segmented, *See* Portes and
    Rumbaut
social systems' influence
    on, 5
theory, early use of, 9
theory, seven dimensions
    of. *See* Gordon
theory, use for recent ethnic
    immigrants. *See* Alba
    and Nee
theory, viewed as
    ideologically laden, 11
Basch, 12, 13, 15, 115, 122
Bassey, 116
Bell, 126
Benson, 3, 4, 5, 12, 141
Berry and Phinney, 2, 5
Biko, 116
Black American narrative, 115
Black Caribbean immigrants, 6,
    141, 142, 144
Black racial consciousness, 130,
    131
Black racial status. *See* Blacks